ENNEAGRAM II

ENNEAGRAM II

Advancing Spiritual Discernment

RICHARD ROHR

A Crossroad Book
The Crossroad Publishing Company
New York

This printing: 2000

The Crossroad Publishing Company
370 Lexington Avenue, New York, NY 10017

Printed in the United States of America

Library of Congress Cataloging-in-Publication Data

Rohr, Richard.
    Enneagram II : advancing spiritual discernment / Richard Rohr.
      p. cm.
    Includes index.
    ISBN 0-8245-1451-3; 0-8245-1766-0 (pbk.)
    1. Spiritual life—Catholic Church. 2. Enneagram. 3. Spiritual
Exercises. I. Title. II. Title: Enneagram 2.
BX2350.2.R642   1995
248.2—dc20   94-41710

To all those whom I loved poorly,
Because I am a ONE,
To all those who loved me anyway,
Despite my being a ONE,
Trusting mercy from the first,
Offering immense gratitude to the second.
All waiting for the Hidden Wholeness,
Who alone is a Perfect TEN.

First the fall,
and then the recovery from the fall,
but *both* are the Mercy of God.

—*Julian of Norwich*

One should not repent too much.
The value of sin is very great.

—*Meister Eckhart*

Why do you call me good?
God alone is good.

—*Jesus to the rich young man*

Where sin abounds,
grace abounds even more.

—*Paul to the Romans, 5:21*

Contents

Part III
Discussion of the Types in Action

Preface

We present this book with some trepidation because, as some people move deeper into dynamic processes like the Enneagram, it often happens that knowledge overtakes experience. My concern for these people is that for these people the information they receive about the Enneagram might be moving them forward at a rate faster and deeper than their experience can deal with. If the Enneagram were merely a clever scheme for categorizing people or a stimulating intellectual game, I would be far less concerned about the consequences of what I write. I would also probably not be writing this book. The Enneagram, however, is a very powerful spiritual tool. And it can be truly profitable as the conversion tool it was meant to be only if, somehow, the reader's experience is at least keeping pace with the information.

Usually, I discuss this material only in individual spiritual direction, where I can get feedback at each step along the way and guide the process in dialogue with the other person.

Nevertheless, it is important and valuable to present the Enneagram as I believe it was meant to be presented, as a tool for conversion. Therefore, as you read these pages I ask you to study and reflect on the Enneagram not just as an interesting tool for self-knowledge, but as a tool for the transformation of consciousness. It is primarily food for the soul.

When the wisdom of the Enneagram is encountered as it should be, it produces nothing less than that — a spiritual revolution. In this light, I'd like to offer some orientation with a quote from Paul's letter to the Ephesians. I believe these words were meant to be pondered right here at the beginning:

> You must give up your old way of life, you must put aside your old self which gets corrupted by following illusory desires. Your mind must be renewed by a spiritual revolution. (Eph. 4:22–23)

I recently gave an Enneagram workshop to a team of psychologists and counselors. During the second day, the head of a major counseling center came to me and described how he had awakened during the night with an entirely new perspective on himself. "I really thought I knew myself," he said to me, "and I've been counseling and guiding all sorts of people for years. I will never be the same after what I saw at four o'clock this morning. My whole life and all my major decisions I now see through another prism. I was never able to perceive things in this way before."

This comes from a man who for years had done much inner work and had counseled many other people.

That's why we must honor the Enneagram as a tool of spiritual revolution.

The biblical word for spiritual conversion is *revolutio* (a "turning completely around") in Latin and *metanoia* (a "change of heart") in Greek. That turning around of the heart is what we're talking about here.

Unfortunately, what Americans did to the Enneagram when it was first discovered was what we do to almost everything in our country: we made it into an interesting piece of psychologizing. The widespread misrepresentation of the Enneagram as merely a psychological tool and the nonrecognition of its spiritually revolutionary power disappoint me.

I want to emphasize that the Enneagram is not primarily a tool of the mind, but a tool of the soul. The goal and direction of the Enneagram is spiritual conversion. There is no way through it without the experience of abandonment to grace.

If you try to "do" it — if you try to make it happen by reading more books on the Enneagram — it's not going to transform your soul. If you focus only on studying it more, which FIVEs are wont to do, it will just move you more into ego-consciousness. And what you end up doing is attacking your FIVE with FIVE energy or attacking your EIGHT with EIGHT energy, which merely makes the problem worse.

You need to approach the Enneagram process as a spiritual revolution, a conversion experience.

In addition to those who misuse the Enneagram, there are those who would like to sweep it away. For example, there are some religious groups, mostly conservative ones, who have recently become very critical of the Enneagram. One reason might be that such people often define conversion as a "pious" event that revolves around one's choice of denominational affiliation or worship style or a preferred type of Jesus language.

The Enneagram, however, talks about a conversion of such scope and magnitude that, in effect, it says, "You must change, or even better, you must *be* changed at a most profound level."

If people are not ready to change their life and question their motivation, they're not ready for the Enneagram at all. Such people would prefer to condemn it, even without understanding it. Only dogs bark at what they *don't* know; humans have the God-given gift of knowing — and then deciding whether they need to "bark."

But it seems to me that the business of the churches is precisely conversion. Isn't that what religion has always talked about? You would think that any tool designed to help individuals recognize how the ego avoids truth and how the ego avoids God would be most welcome by religious people, but that's apparently not always the case.

Let me return to Paul. He continues,

> Your mind must be renewed by a spiritual revolution so you can put on a new self that has been created in God's way, in the goodness and holiness of truth. So, from now on, there must be no more lies. (Eph. 4:24–25)

By the way, Paul's not talking only to THREEs in this letter; he's talking to all of us. From now on, for every one of us, there must be no more lies.

The lie is what we're all trapped in, as you find out when you study the Enneagram and learn who you are.

As you read the following pages, I am assuming that you are familiar with the Enneagram and its dynamics and that you already know your number. If you are unfamiliar with the Enneagram, please refer to the Appendix on p. 184 or consult any of the various introductory books on the Enneagram, such as my *Discovering the Enneagram: An Ancient Tool for a New Spiritual Journey* (New York: Crossroad, 1990).

It should be noted that *Enneagram II* was originally presented as a living workshop, and that is both its strength and its weakness. One must read it as the dialogical-oral experience that Enneagram teaching was meant to be. But readers will not find here the linear formality that many are more comfortable with. It is only due to the patience and editing and genius of Lou Savary that it has become a book at all. Please thank him for the clarity and blame me, Richard, for any incompleteness or confusion. As I say throughout this book, my gift is also my greatest curse.

Part I

Paths to God

1

Discovering the Truth about Ourselves

We're all — each Enneagram number — trapped in a false idea of God. We're all trapped in a false idea of sin, too. Moreover, I find that even those of us who are serious about the spiritual life are often attacking wrong sins and aiming at wrong virtues. That's why the Enneagram is so enlightening.

It produces in us a spiritual revolution, because it turns our lives around. This begins to happen when we realize we've been trapped in a great disguise, or what Paul calls a "lie."

"You must speak the truth to one another since we are all parts of one another" (Eph. 4:25). What a beautiful line! That "we are all parts of one another" is exactly what we hope the Enneagram has taught us. Yet not only that we are parts of one another, but also that we are parts of something much bigger than ourselves. In fact, the only thing we can be is a part of that bigger something, never the whole of it. This is the truth we must speak.

Another truth is that I'm trapped in my ONEness, and you are trapped in your number. Even though I'm trying to learn how to let God make grace and life out of my ONEness, I will always be a ONE.

Another truth is that in my ONEness I reflect part of the glory and goodness of God. But I've also learned to recognize that you reflect part of God's glory in your number too.

(That's probably just the way a ONE would say it, because we ONEs all want everybody else to be glorious and "good"! We want everyone to look at life from our perspective of perfection.)

The Enneagram and Community

I want to repeat now what I know to be true: Enneagram conversion makes you less judgmental than you were, more "spacious" and more accessible.

If you haven't become less judgmental, then the conversion has not happened for you.

3

Converted people hold themselves lightly and leave room for change and growth. They are therefore capable of community. Others can get in, and they can get out — of themselves.

Your ability to accept me frees me; I hope to do the same for you and for every other. I think the Enneagram process could and should make community very possible. I mean community in the deepest and truest sense, where people are empty enough of themselves to make room for the other, where I hold a place in my heart for the one who is not like me.

I've known the Enneagram now for twenty years. I've said it before but I want to say it here: The depth and truth of it continues to astound me. I continue to see in deeper ways that I am a ONE and in deeper ways how my sin disguises itself.

As I get older, my sin gets more sophisticated, more complex. If I don't catch it "on the run," I normally don't catch it at all. Once I get on the conveyor belt taking my sin with me, I can't see it and I usually have to have someone else from the side point it out to me: "Richard, you're doing it again."

This is one reason why we need one another for our spiritual growth. We each need a truth-teller who says to us, "You're doing it again, you're slipping into it, you're losing it, you're caught on the conveyor belt."

A Mystery to Ourselves

For the most part, we don't know how to get off the conveyor belt. And we each have our own form of conveyor belt. I believe we are all an infinite mystery to ourselves.

I quote the German Jesuit Karl Rahner:

The faith it takes to accept the infinite mystery that you are, and the faith it takes to accept the infinite mystery that God is, are finally the same act of faith.

I would add that the acceptance of both mysteries — who I am and who God is — moves forward in parallel order.

The Enneagram is designed to increase our ability to accept the personal mystery, to answer the question: "Why do I do these things?"

We've all found our styles of getting attention — not getting the attention of other people, but getting our own attention. Those self-attention-getting styles are so deep in us now that we don't know any other way to do it. I don't think this style really ever changes in an individual. That's why most of the teachers of the Enneagram insist you're trapped in one capital sin and you're bound to that one capital sin forever. My experience says that this is almost always true.

The original concept of a capital sin goes back to the first millennium of Christianity, perhaps specifically to Gregory the Great, who enumerated seven major ways of being trapped in sin. So the idea of capital sins is not something new. As you know, whoever first developed the Enneagram added two more major sins — deceit and anxiety — to the traditional seven deadlies.

A Tool for Discernment

The Enneagram may also be used as what I would call today a "tool for discernment." We aren't taught much about discernment these days, and I think that's why some people on the religious right are so threatened by the Enneagram. The ages-long tradition of discernment, which has always been very strong in the Catholic Church, especially in the Ignatian Jesuit tradition, is something to which many of our people have hardly been exposed. And yet throughout the centuries, discernment has always been crucial and central in spiritual direction.

For example, you can't get much more orthodox than someone like Catherine of Siena. In her *Dialogues,* she pictures the spiritual life as a large tree.

First of all, the *trunk of the tree* is love.

Next, Catherine says, the *core of the tree* — the middle that has to be alive for the rest of the tree to be alive — is *patience.* Isn't that a surprise? For Catherine, no virtue happens unless you have patience with yourself.

The *roots of the tree* — now this isn't Freud or Jung writing, this is Catherine of Siena — the roots that sustain the whole tree she identifies as *self-knowledge.* You will not grow in love, she claims, without self-knowledge.

What are the *branches of the tree* of the spiritual life? What reaches out to connect us to the larger world? *Discernment.* Only when you have discernment, she claims, do you know how to listen, how to weigh the inner and outer voices, how to hear deeply what is happening in relationships.

In other words, according to Catherine, love does not happen without self-knowledge, without patience and without discernment.

These three virtues are not big-ticket items in churches today, and because we are without them we pay heavily. For example, without these three, people mostly enter into co-dependency instead of love, and there is no solid trunk to the tree of life. A major psychological discovery, made largely in the last ten years, is that much of what we've called "love" has really been co-dependence.

If you think we Americans are a discerning people, we have a national example to show how we're not: the Persian Gulf War. Researchers reported that just one day before this war began, 80 percent of the American people were against it. Yet only one day after the war began, when it looked like it would be a quick victory, 80 percent were for it!

Now, these statistics tell me clearly that, when the real issues arise, there is no discernment going on in America. Apparently there's no spiritual discernment even possible. There's just collectivist thinking. Whatever the mass consciousness is, even our Catholic people with all their years of Catholic education and religious development by and large slip into it.

So the tree of the spiritual life does not grow strong without the roots of self-knowledge. Self-knowledge helps us really understand why we do what we do. It shows us the prisms and biases through which all of us look at reality, and it monitors those branches reaching out to the sun that bring in the data for discernment.

In the most traditional teaching on discernment, it says that discernment is not possible (and remember, the Enneagram is about discernment) without a deep and honest desire to know the truth. If that desire is not there, you can't discern. At best, you'll do prudential decision-making.

That means you'll base your decisions largely on what's reasonable, what's functional, and what works. If our side is winning the war, it must be moral. If it looks like everybody is for it, it must be okay. This is not discernment, but following the crowd. At best, it means merely finding appropriate answers or merely resolving a problem.

Discernment is not problem-solving. True discernment is not possible unless there is total abandonment to grace. Now, I don't know if such abandonment is fully possible to humans, but at least we can ask for that grace: total abandonment to the Spirit.

When you work on a discernment process with someone in spiritual direction, until they've come to a point of abandonment to God's grace, saying, "I'm ready, Lord, to go this way or to go that way, to go backward or to go forward; I just want to do your will," true discernment is not possible.

We are unable to go forward spiritually unless there is in us a willingness to abandon to God, to surrender, to let go — whatever word for "abandonment to grace" your tradition makes you comfortable with.

Without abandonment to God, we will not even want conversion or be willing to turn our lives around. We will be content to go to church services and adhere to a few self-chosen mandates.

These are deep questions and they have no easy answers.

Although the traditional Twelve Step program told us to trust in a power outside ourselves, there's a new school within the Twelve Step movement that wants to revise the step that acknowledges a divine power to now read, "I want to trust the higher power within myself." I have problems with that.

In America, we tend to turn things back into the private self. Instead of turning to a One "out there" that I can surrender to, trust, call upon, yell at — whatever it might be — we prefer to find everything inside us, inside ME.

What this self-focused attitude makes impossible is relationship with the rest of reality. Without relationship to others, it's just a process of going inside and messing around with my feelings.

That's *not* what we're doing in the Enneagram.

Working with the Enneagram is, of course, going to raise up some feelings. I'm sure some of them will be feelings you don't like to see within yourself.

But the question for us is always, "What are the feelings for?"

So you got in touch with your grief. So what? You got in touch with your anger. So what? You got in touch with your fear. So what? If the most sophisticated phrase you use is, "Oh, he's really in touch," well, that's fine as far as it goes. But the spiritual question still remains: "What is 'being in touch' for the sake of?"

The answer is: "It's always for the sake of love." We are created for communion.

For me, the Enneagram is all about growing in love. There is no other goal on this earth except to grow in love. Spirituality is always about love. Always. I want to present the Enneagram in that light.

Our task in discernment is to sift through appearances and the many ambiguities of our life situations, and from among the various alternatives, decisions, or choices, to discover where the truth is.

More precisely, *discernment is to discover where the truth is for me.* I don't want you to read this phrase "where the truth is for me" in a cheap individualistic way, because I believe with all my heart that creation is already redemption. Let me explain that.

I believe it is good Genesis theology — it is certainly good Franciscan theology — that already in the act of creation, *God has named you.* God has established who you shall be. In the act of creation, your you-ness is hard-wired into the core of your being, your essence is already imprinted there.

Our Franciscan philosopher Duns Scotus called "you-ness" the "thisness" of things, the *haecceity* (pronounced "hake-SEE-i-ty) of

things. He said that God created only individuals, that's all. God
did not create genus and species. God created you and you and
you *as you*. In all truth, I believe profoundly now, not out of some
head conviction but out of experience in working with people, that
the spiritual life is a matter of becoming who you truly are. Not
becoming Catherine of Siena, but becoming who you truly are.

The poet Gerard Manley Hopkins was totally enamored with Scotus's understanding of individual creation and the "thisness" of each
thing. In "Inversnaid" he expressed it as only a poet can:

> Each mortal thing does one thing and the same:
> Deals out that being indoors each one dwells;
> Selves — goes itself: myself it speaks and spells,
> Crying *What I do is me: for that I came.*
>
> I say more: the just man justices;
> Keeps grace: that keeps all his goings graces;
> Acts in God's eye what in God's eye he is —
> Christ — for Christ plays in ten thousand places,
> Lovely in limbs, and lovely in eyes not his
> To the Father through the features of men's faces.

Like few Christians, Duns Scotus and Hopkins took the Christian
doctrines of creation and incarnation to their entirely necessary
conclusion. It is to our shame that so few others have done the same.

Now when people hear this truth, it may sound superficial: "Oh,
that sounds easy; I'll just go out and be myself tonight." The way
Americans use the phrase "be myself" is not what I'm talking about.
To be who you truly are is work.

At Our Core

All the great world traditions of religion talk about a conflict
between essence and personality.

The word "personality," as you may know, comes from the Greek
word *persona*, which means "mask." This is what Thomas Merton
calls the "false self" — all of the personal and social stuff we put
on and live up to, the roles we carry out in society thinking that they
define who we truly are.

You may call your "essence" your "center" or your "soul" or
whatever you want.

The great religious traditions remind us that there is some deviation at our core. This deviation is certainly at the core of our
personality, because the personality is all window dressing anyway,

but it's even found at the core of our essence (although it does not destroy the essence, which is still created in the image of God). The biblical word for that essential deviation is "sin." Even at the essence of who we are, there is some inability to be it, to trust it, to act out of it.

Now, the fact is that we have some willfulness in that sin; there has been some decision on our part in shaping that core. I can look back to when I was a child and say that I didn't know the process or I was too little to be responsible for my sin. But there was a time, already as a little boy, I think, when I decided to be a ONE. The proclivity was there, the readiness was there, the personality was partially there.

But there was also a decision on my part to be a ONE. This century has whittled away at the great mystery of free will, but we have also lost human dignity as a result.

Can you sense a similar decision in your own life to be your own Enneagram number?

Somewhere, my ONEness started working for me. Somewhere, it won friends and influenced people. Somewhere, it made me look like a white knight. I cleaned the blackboard for the nuns and they gave me an award afterwards. When I found out that being a "good boy" worked, I decided, "Why not keep doing it?"

That's what we mean by the biblical concept of sin: At our very core, there is still a lie. (For me, the lie is: I am a "good boy.") And until that lie is healed, surrendered, let go of, abandoned as unnecessary, and forgotten as ridiculous, we will keep living *through* it and from *within* it. This lie prevents us from being able to surrender to the self that we truly are and to the God who truly is.

The goal of all spiritual direction is to bring the true person before the true God, the naked person before the naked God. A good spiritual director is always trying to bring "who you really are" before "who God really is."

That's a terrifying journey! It requires in a director good spirituality and psychology on one side, and good theology on the other, to be able to give you not only who God truly is but also who you truly are.

The reason I have found so much fruit in the Enneagram is that it has the ability to open up both sides of that relationship.

Not only does the Enneagram show you who you truly are, but it can also help open up the experience of God as God really is. The Enneagram does not present the distorted images of God that we might be addicted to and that religion often gives to us. I find that many people worship, to use our contemporary word, a dysfunctional God. A clearly dysfunctional God, for example, is a God who's undercutting them, who's against them, who's making it impossible for them to love.

And that is the true definition of sin. Whatever is making it impossible for you to love or whatever is making it impossible for other people to love, that's sin.

Of course, there are many ways we make it impossible to love.

2

Working Together with God

Some people think it is new and trendy to talk about a "spiritual journey" and "stages" of a spiritual journey. For those of you who are Catholic, all you have to do is look on both side walls of your church and you'll see the Stations of the Cross. The Stations were conceived of as milestones of a spiritual journey; they marked stages of surrendering, of dying, and of understanding. They were intended to describe stages of entering into darkness and re-entering into light.

Many of us in college had to read Dante's *Divine Comedy*. The work is structured as a spiritual journey. As Dante led us into the *inferno* — into hell, into illusion, into darkness — he illustrated all the capital sins in the various levels of hell.

Notice, Dante doesn't have God torturing anybody, as many people have falsely supposed, or God kicking people into the pit. Rather, in each case, evil is presented as its own punishment.

Take vanity, for example. People who spent their whole lives living up to their image with fancy clothes and social prestige are imprisoned in the pit of hell because they are burdened by wearing huge loads of heavy clothes. They can't move from one place to another because they are rendered immobile by the weight of so many clothes on their backs.

And pride. Pride-filled people are stuck in huge ice-pits at the bottom of hell; they're frozen cold and hard for all eternity. Their pride brought them to hell already frozen: separate, superior, self-sufficient, with no willingness to "melt" or "sweat."

The Providence of God

Dante is telling us again and again that people choose their own death, while God is asking us to choose life. For Dante, God is saying, "I am trying to call you beyond death to love."

That is what I think the Christian tradition means by the providence of God. It's a word I'm sure you've heard, but today it has taken on a rather pious or unreal connotation. What the tradition means by the providence of God can be best described by locating it between two extremes.

11

On the one hand, there's the major theological position of "predestination." Many construe this belief to mean that God has planned every little thing in your life from all eternity. You hear this approach spoken of a lot today: "God has a divine plan for your life." What they mean by that is we're sort of puppets on a string and everything we say and do is predestined and predetermined. All we do is just live it out. This approach may also be named "fatalism." Most people wouldn't admit to this belief, but in many lives it is still operative.

At the other extreme is the belief called deism. Most of the founders of this country — Washington, Jefferson — were deists. They saw, as they put it, the collection of humans and the whole world much like a mechanical clock all wound up and ticking itself out. According to this scenario, in the beginning God cranked up the big mechanical clock then put it aside and went off in the heavens doing God's own thing. Meantime, we were left to fight it out down here. And even though we're all just parts of a wound-up clock, we're still responsible for the results that happen on earth. It's all up to us. The deism approach to reality has infected America to this day. We still believe basically that *we* have to make it happen. The deistic belief is one reason why we're so success-oriented in this country. We believe that if we don't make it happen, if we don't get it together, it's not going to happen.

Predestination and deism are the two extremes: predestination puts excessive reliance on so-called grace and deism puts excessive reliance on self-responsibility.

Now, locate divine providence right in the middle of those two.

Probably providence is expressed nowhere better than in Romans 8:28, where it says, "God works together with." The Greek word here is *synergia* (pronounced "sin-er-GEE-uh") and means "gives energy with." God cooperates *with* people to bring about good. God will work together with any person who seeks the good.

Can you imagine that such a relationship with God could really be true? That every moment God is trying to expand your freedom? That, at this very instant, God is trying to make this choice you're now making a choice that is more alive, more vital, clearer, truer? And that God is even using your mistakes and sins to bring about good?

I believe all of these incredible claims are profoundly true. I believe this synergy is what the providence of God is all about. God is working for our wholeness, our liberation, our truth, and our freedom probably more than we are. What we can do is keep saying, "Yes, I want it. I want life, I want freedom, I want truth, I want the real. Keep me 'little.' Keep me out of the driver's seat, so we can cooperate, so we can 'work together with' as partners." If that's not the providence of God, what else could the providence of God be?

Co-creation spirituality, which enjoys a longstanding tradition among the Judaeo-Christian people, provides another way of look-ing at divine providence: God and we as a team are both working together. The most surprising — perhaps to us the most scandaliz-ing — point is that God uses our passions and our compulsions in our favor! God uses even our sins for divine purposes. Nothing is wasted in God's Great Economy.

I think this is the spirituality that the Enneagram is trying to ex-press: how the providence of God works to make *all* things work out for good" (Rom. 8:28).

The Gift of Our Passions

The goal is not to get rid of our passions. The Enneagram empha-sizes our passions as blessings. This shift in emphasis is the gift of the Enneagram, the gift of each of the numbers.

I believe God uses our compulsiveness for our freedom, so don't concentrate on "getting rid of it." For example, as a ONE, I needn't try hard to get rid of my anger. What each of us must learn to do with our compulsion is three things: *Hold it, observe it, and trust the best part of it.* Let's look at each of these three steps.

First, *hold it.* Don't try to dismiss your passion too quickly; don't try to judge it too quickly. For example, when as a ONE I get angry, I should just let it be there, saying, "Okay, I'm angry again; there it is." It's important not to deny its reality either and pretend I'm not angry, as we ONEs often do. When you're into your compulsion, just hold it right there.

Second, *observe it.* Don't run from it, don't get on the conveyor belt so you can pretend it's not happening. Look at it. Study its texture, its form, its shape, its source, its goal. Ask yourself some penetrating questions such as, "Where did my passion come from and where is it going? Why am I acting this way? Why am I angry? Why am I re-sentful? Why am I judgmental? Is this coming from my essence, from the center? Or is it coming from the surface, the personality and its protective layer? Is my compulsion really protecting some righteous cause that matters, or is just my little ego feeling offended? Or is it just my way of doing things or my 'right' way of perceiving things?" Hold it, observe it, and then —

Third, *trust the best part of it.* You'll know the difference if you've observed your compulsion long enough. Once you've held it and stayed with it, you'll notice that some of it just rolls away. Or, like a cobweb, you can blow some of it off your hand. With experience, you learn to recognize, "This is not real. This doesn't truly matter. Why would I live within it? Why would I protect it?" What I am asking you here is to live out of the best part of your compulsion. Hold it, observe it, and trust the best part of it.

God uses your style of attention for divine purposes. God uses *your* style — FOUR, FIVE, SIX, or whatever — to bring about a style of life that is greater than the sum of its broken parts. Maybe that's why we call it transformation or "divine alchemy."

The Dark Night

The history of spirituality reflects two arms of God's love. One is the right arm, which we've tended to trust. This corresponds to the providence of God as I've already described it: God is working with us, providing energy for us, making life out of what we screw up, making freedom out of our lies. "You're sixty years old and you're still doing your compulsion," says God. "Let's make life out of it." That's the right arm of God.

But there is another arm of God. The left hand of God has been an even harder side of God to trust. Let's just call it the painful mystery of things, the ambiguity of things, the nonsensical character of things, the paradox that you are.

If you don't like this contemporary language of ambiguity and paradox, use Teresa of Avila's language of "journey" through the rooms of the "interior castle."

She talked about stages. She talked about capital sins that had to be recognized, one after another, especially the one that held her heart tight. She said the journey to God took her through great darkness; it was the dark night of the soul.

St. John of the Cross described two kinds of dark nights for the soul: the dark night of the senses and the dark night of the spirit. They each followed different rules and came at different times. Hardly anybody knows how to identify these dark nights today or understands how they prepare us for "dawn."

One slight criticism I have of the Twelve Step programs is related to this. Sometimes people are being led by grace into the dark night of the senses and it is misperceived even by the movement's leaders. Some Twelve Step programs can be too oriented toward problem-solving, toward getting through it, doing the steps, "You're not doing the steps!" Maybe the person is doing the steps perfectly, while at the same time something entirely different is happening in that person's soul, and it goes unrecognized.

The dark night is part of purgation and purification. That's not just medieval Catholic language. *Purgatorio* is a stage you must go through to let go of the lie.

The dark night of the senses is primarily a purgatory experience; it involves letting go of the false self. So for a while during your purgatory, your senses give false signals; they don't work. More than anything else, they just dry up.

The temptation is to move right in there to quickly solve the problem — to get out of that dark night and to get back into familiar sensations and feelings, good feelings especially. Americans always need to feel good about themselves.

The truth is that you have to go through the dark night, you have to endure a period in which your feelings don't make a bit of sense. You don't like having them because they're not positive; they're not telling you you're good or even that life is good. Instead, they are leading you into places of meaninglessness. It is important to pass through these places on your journey.

We desperately need spiritual direction that teaches us to walk through that kind of terrain and trust it. Or better: *hold it, observe it, and trust the good part of it.* Those who can help us through the dark night are the great teachers. Those who say the dark night must be avoided or that it is always the result of sin or some problem are not good teachers at all.

Great Teachers

I believe your passion, as well as your capital sin, is also a great teacher.

Joy is a teacher to SEVENs, but they better go all the way with their joy: taste the edges of it and every part of it and discover where joy finally leads them. They must learn that they can't hold on to that joy; they can't make it happen day after day after day.

To us ONEs, anger is a great teacher.

Passion is a teacher to you EIGHTs. But go all the way with your passion.

That may sound terribly dangerous to some people because, as overly religious people, we've been trained to cut passion off. We have learned to stop the flow, normally, by a judgment or by categorizing. (Judging always involves putting something in a category.)

It has taken me a long time to recognize that judgment is usually employed as a means of control. Judgment is a control technique that the ego likes because it makes us feel secure again. Even if your judgment condemns you, you would sooner make that judgment than not, in order to put things in their place, to label people and situations, and to know where life is at.

I see myself being judgmental far too often. And I know it is not of God. I have observed it. When in the past I acted judgmentally, it gave me a righteous, secure, ordered feeling. Making a judgment may have satisfied the needs of my personality, but not the essence of who I really am. The essence can let things like that just be. The essence can let all things be. The essence can trust is-ness. It can trust what is, and affirm that what is is okay.

Everything that *is* is okay: darkness and light.

In Catholic theology, the word for the okayness of everything is the "paschal mystery." It affirms that half of life is death and half is resurrection. You cannot avoid either half, not even if you move to Hawaii.

On a recent visit to that enchanted land, I told the participants in a big international Christian conference about the dark night of the soul, and it was new language to many of them. I said, "Even here, in the midst of all this beauty and sunshine, don't think there's any place you can dwell that you're not going to have to face the dark side. You can't run away from it."

Ironically, a lot of us religious folk have a problem with the bright side of the paschal mystery. Many of us have a hard time trusting the resurrection. We have a hard time trusting ecstasy. We have a hard time trusting joy or freedom.

We believe that, somehow, freedom's always going to lead us to deviance. SIXes especially believe that the exercise of human freedom will only get them into trouble.

We fear taking responsibility for our soul, because we can't trust providence. We can't trust that God is working together with us, giving us enough energy to turn around "all things unto good." Read it in Romans 8:28.

"All things" includes the dark things. Darkness is a great teacher. The *inferno* has to be walked through; it offers us important lessons. In this regard, Robert Bly is making some important points in the men's movement. For example, he points out how initiation rites for men in almost all primitive civilizations always lead the man to go down — down into the ashes, into some kind of ritual circumcision, ritual humiliation.

It's always there in the initiation rites, ritually humiliating those who feel they're on the top.

The same is not true for women. In a patriarchal culture where women are on the bottom, normally the initiation invitation for women is just the opposite: "Come up. Trust the ecstasy. Trust your body. Trust yourself. Trust your intuition. Come up. Come up."

You can read the entire gospel as a two-directional invitation. It's either, "Come down" or "Come up." To those on the top Jesus is saying, as to the rich young man, "Come down. Give it all away. Let go. Come down." To those on the bottom, Jesus is saying, as to the Syro-Phoenician woman who was a nobody sitting on the edge of life with her hemorrhage, "Come on up. Up higher. Go show yourself to the priests. You're better than any of them."

Two different kinds of good news in one gospel. I think the Enneagram, if it is rightly understood, has the power to help us to move in both directions, as needed: to pull us up, to help us trust the passion and the gift that is there; and also to call us down, to counter a false sense of being on top when necessary, to remind us of the sin at our core.

We all need the two-way movement, the paschal mystery. Some call it the *yin* and the *yang*. (I'm sure when I use those words from East Asian traditions, I will upset some people who will then think that the Enneagram is occult.)

When Fear Barks

I should mention that some people are criticizing the Enneagram because they say it is from non-Christian sources. First of all, in truth, no matter what they say in books, even what I say in my book, we really don't know where the Enneagram came from. Some say the Sufis gave it to the world, but that's only as far as we can trace it today. Some researchers claim that its sources go farther back than that. We really don't know where it came from.

But suppose it came from non-Christian sources; should that be a rule for discarding it? If Christians threw out everything that came from non-Christian sources, we'd easily lose three quarters of the Bible, including the entire Old Testament, since that's from a Jewish source. Next, we'd have to drop the "Logos," the Word of God, in John's Gospel, since its source was Greek philosophy. And so on.

I want to point this out because if you become involved with the Enneagram, you will surely be faced with this kind of criticism. People are saying the Enneagram is occult, it's pagan, it's non-Christian, it's New Age. (New Age is currently the umbrella word some people use to cover everything they're afraid of.)

I remember a wise old Franciscan theology teacher. "Richard," he said, "an awful lot of people are like dogs. They bark at everything they don't know."

Barking is one way fear shows itself; that's the way SIXes show themselves, for instance. But it's not just SIXes who are doing this fearful barking today. As I often say, it's the SIX energy that's loose in America, the SIX demon that's running around and barking all over in our society.

Look at the Persian Gulf War! Where did that come from?

The SIX demon.

Were we really protecting America? Where was protection really needed?

In America, everything is seen through that SIX prism of security and fear. The reason wars always have to be fought, we tell ourselves, is to make ourselves safe. We see war as a matter of self-protection.

I'm going to hit the demon of fear pretty hard, as I did in *Discovering the Enneagram*, because it's on the loose. First of all, we've got to name it more accurately than "protection." At the same time, I want to help us discover the gift that is also present in that fear.

Repentance

One tradition of conversion says people are converted in three ways, by three paths. And we each tend to stay on one path or another, whichever one we're on.

First, some are converted by the *embrace of the lover*. Second, others are converted by the *blood of the hero*. Third, others are converted by the *tears of repentance*.

This tradition says we have to go along one of those three paths — love, blood, or tears — in order to be converted. Each way teaches us how to stay on our path.

The blood of the hero, by the way, refers to the classic path of martyrdom. Other terms to describe it include the way of sacrifice, the way of giving, the way of surrender, the way of letting go.

This three-path tradition goes on to say that the first two paths — love and blood — will never work until we've tried the third.

Without repentance, the embrace of the lover will probably turn out to be false love — "co-dependency" we say today. It will be two people sucking energy from one another, leaning on one another, but having no clarity, no ground, no authority, no autonomy with which to grace one another.

Without repentance, the blood of the hero can be shed for all the wrong heroic, patriotic reasons.

In other words, the embrace of the lover and the blood of the hero will probably not lead you all the way through to wholeness and holiness without the tears of repentance.

One gift of the Enneagram is to help you cry, to help you weep over your sin. I sincerely mean that. I'm not using poetic language here.

Until you come to that point when you realize how many people you've hurt and how you've kept your own self back from truth and light by your own sin, so that you almost want to cry over it, you either have not got the right number (some people don't — they're still looking at the wrong sin) or you haven't seen how bad the sin is, how really dark it can be, and how much it can keep you from God and the truth.

3

The Many Paths to God

In recent months, I have become fascinated with a new understanding of "the path." I'm going to try to explain it as best I can. Then I'd like to use this new understanding as a take-off point for the rest of the book.

I believe that God has made each of us as an individual, unrepeatable creation. I recognize that God has obviously given us different temperaments, different personalities, different families and cultures. As a result, I see clearly that God has given each of us a different set of glasses through which to look at life. So when God places us at such different starting points with such utterly different inner and outer lives to begin our journey, there is no way God can be demanding that we all follow a uniform path.

Enneagram means "the nine points," the nine fundamental viewpoints. So it offers at least nine paths.

There is, of course, a problem with having many paths — and there are far more than nine paths — including the confusion around discernment and choice of the path to follow. But there is another problem in the spiritual life that revolves around a lack of trust in the path that is ours.

I think the problem is not that we don't have a certain basic trust in our path; the problem is that most of us don't *fully* trust our path. Most of us don't really go all the way with it, trusting all of its stages, its dark nights, its ecstasies and all its lessons in between.

Like everyone else, I look at people on this earth and make generalizations about what I see. But as a preacher, I'm always looking from the eyes of my priestly bias, asking myself, "How can I help them understand the spiritual way?" And I meet people who speak with utter sincerity and good will, but I discover they have a completely different set of assumptions built into themselves that are not mine.

I don't believe that it's my place to try to change them. That's part of my new understanding of "the path." Let me try to explain.

The Preeminent Path

I do believe as a Christian that the preeminent path is profoundly named by Jesus. I'm going to call the preeminent path the way of littleness. That is, persons begin walking this preeminent path when they get to the point where they see that the truth of life is in little-ness, in poverty of spirit, in brokenness, in simplicity, in the edges of things, in the bottoms of things. When on this path of littleness, a person is led to live with a universal trust in all life and to respect life wherever it may be. Today, we in the church call this path the "seamless garment." Some of you may name it "nonviolence."

That's why Christ is called "divine revelation." Revelation means some awareness you would never come to by logic. For example, you would never by logic and reason come to the conclusion that the truth is found in the brokenness of things, in the edges of things and in the bottoms of things. Human reason alone would not lead you there. Revelation and reason are two different things. Christ is a revelation. Notice, we call him Lamb of God. The truth is found not in the Lion, but in the Lamb, in a place you would not expect to find truth.

I believe the way of littleness and the way of nonviolence is the way of Jesus. It marks the final mile of everyone's journey.

I can picture many other paths, all of which lead up to the pre-eminent path, including the nine paths that we call the Enneagram. I believe there are many other good, helpful, and necessary paths that people have to walk, and they will find their way if only they walk their special path with total trust.

Some of the paths that lead up to the preeminent path are not nec-essarily "Christian," but they're necessary for certain people. You must allow such people to follow those paths, because those paths are uniquely their paths and not yours. It is not your right or your responsibility to detour them from their paths. Rather, you can in-vite them to trust their paths fully, because if they walk their paths all the way, they will come to the preeminent path. They will come to see that truth lives in the edges of things, in what is broken and poor.

Let me name some of the other likely paths.

Many Paths

The Path of Mysticism. Let me begin with one that to many people looks like the preeminent path. I'll call it the path of mysticism. I think some people, FIVEs especially, are inclined to the path of mys-ticism. I don't think, as such, it is the Jesus path. I don't see Jesus teaching breathing exercises or how to get in touch with your center

and focus your attention. Jesus is living in this world. He incorpo-
rates the mystical path. You would never call Jesus a mystic in the
tradition of classical mystics like Teresa of Avila or John of the Cross.

I'm glad for Teresa of Avila and glad for John of the Cross, but in a
certain way they've made that path impossible for the rest of us who
just can't seem to do it their way. Is that the preeminent path, to do
what Teresa did? It's a fine path, and those on it are gifted for it, but
I don't see it as the preeminent path.

Many people are called by the path of mysticism. I met a woman
once who, I believe, had a call in her very being to be a mystic, to be
a contemplative in the most profound sense. But she couldn't express
that call, because she was in a disastrous family; she entered into
three horrendous marriages and lived a life of drugs. To look at her,
you would say this woman was a loser. You would say this woman
messed up her life totally and didn't know anything about anything.

I visited that woman several times during the last ten days of her
life. During that final period, providence won. She became a mystic,
a contemplative, a saint. She understood where the truth was and
lived it with glory, peace, and freedom. God triumphed. In those
last few days, God won out and she became what she was meant
to be. To see her in a hospital bed, hardly anyone would name her
as a great woman. Hardly anybody but me knew the beauty of that
woman's soul! Goodness, freedom, surrender, the love of God — it
was all there. I believe her mysticism was just as good as Teresa of
Avila's, but this woman didn't arrive there until the last week of her
fifty-year life.

The Way of Initial Mysticism. I believe there is also a way of initial
mysticism, baby mysticism. I don't mean to be sarcastic. I believe the
charismatic movement offers that initial-mysticism path. It's a good
starting place and a lot of people are called to it. If these people
would just go all the way on that path, they could really become
God-lovers, but many merely keep playing around with the initial
stages. They just keep trumping up feelings; they don't go into the
inferno and the *purgatorio*, so they will never reach the *paradiso*. At
best, what they get is a trumped-up *paradiso*. Paradise-too-quickly is
not paradise. Dante gets there only at the end of the journey.

The Way of Religious Life. Here I'll pick on myself and maybe
some of my readers. We follow the way of religious life, the vows
of monasticism. It's a fine path. I'm on it myself. I don't think it's *the*
way. It obviously isn't. It's just a path that has been very helpful to a
lot of us. It's freed many of us to do some good in the world and to
encounter some truly God-loving people, but it's not necessarily the

path for even a small fraction of people. In fact, the way of religious life poses for many the great danger of keeping us from what I think is the safest path of all.

The Path of Friendship. The path of friendship and relationship is the safest path of all. I'm convinced of it. TWOs can be masters and mistresses of the friendship path; they can be the best. They can also be the absolute worst. I believe loving relationship is the safest path and the path for most people. Just stay with it to the end and it will bring you to the preeminent path. Be faithful and loyal to your relationships, to your commitments, to your loves. They will lead you to the Great Compassion for all that dies and suffers.

The Way of the Artist. I believe there is a path of the artist, the aesthete, the ritualist, the symbolist. FOURs really get into this path. Metaphor is what it's about. "The play's the thing" — but it's not the reality. The play is a path. It's a wonderful path. If you are on this path, don't let anyone label it as un-Christian or unnecessary. God has written in your being what you have to do, the path you are to follow. Keep painting. Keep drawing. Keep writing. Stay on the path of the artist and see where it leads you. I'm sure it can bring you to the preeminent path.

The Erotic Path. This may sound spiritually dangerous to certain people, but I think some people are certainly called to follow the erotic path, the sensual path, the sexual path. For example, the woman mystic I just told you about was on the sexual path most of her life. She listened to it, she suffered from it, it taught her, it whipped her, and she learned it was not God. But it was a way. It was a teacher, a way through. It kept her secure enough long enough to find out what she really desired. That's one advantage of a good sexual relationship. It allows you to be held tightly and warmly long enough to know what you really want. But stay on this path, if it's yours, until it leads you to the path of littleness.

Please don't misunderstand me; I'm not encouraging you to sin. What I am telling you is to recognize your path and observe it; listen to it and learn from it. Again and again, ask yourself: "How can I stay on my path and learn from it? How can I listen to it on all its levels of truth?"

The Way of the Warrior. The warrior is the protector, the defender or boundaries even at cost to self. It's an energy deep in many men and women. And we better understand this special path or we're never going to get rid of war. We desperately need to learn how to redirect the warrior path from its current destructive direction. The East has succeeded in this much better than we have. In the East people have developed the martial arts: where you indeed learn how to kill but you never kill anybody; where you learn not to be afraid of any outer enemy so that you can face the fears and other enemies inside yourself; where you learn to understand the energy, drive, and passion inside yourself. But you never kill. Anyone who doesn't understand that, doesn't understand the martial arts. Sadly, we have almost none of that awareness in the West.

The West has never spiritualized the warrior except for a short period with the Christian knight. It has never taken the protector and defender energy and spiritualized it, except in the realm of religion. Francis of Assisi and Ignatius of Loyola were both knights, both warriors, and they both transferred that wonderful energy into the spiritual life. They became, quite simply, warriors for Christ. They used that same energy to fight for *the* kingdom — the great kingdom of God — instead of the little kingdom of America. But it's still warrior energy. You don't call it bad. You learn how to use it, how to direct it. I believe that's what good spiritual direction today should do.

The Path of Religion. What do you think is the most dangerous path? I think it is the path of religion. From my perspective, the path of law and duty and religion has detoured the erotic, creative, life-giving paths toward God and has pulled many people into a misdirected path of self-serving salvation. Consequently, these people must deal with a self-image that is constantly protecting itself instead of surrendering itself.

I'm saying this as a priest. And I want to be a priest, unless they kick me out. As a priest, I represent religion. I even represent institutional religion and the path of religion. I have to say this path is the best — and it's also the worst.

It's the absolute worst when it leads thousands of people into unhealthy darkness and many other thousands into denial. They're not learning anything from that place of darkness and denial because there's no way through it and no way out of it. Much religion is the maintenance of self-image instead of the scary search for God — saving oneself instead of grace from another.

The path of religion can be dangerous, but it is still a good path. Dangerous doesn't mean it's not good. The religious path provides the words, the symbols, the Scriptures. Without these, I doubt I'd personally have the courage to name the humble, broken, poor part of my own soul. Can you understand the importance of those religious things? Religion gives you the metaphor, the name, and the word for reality, so you can trust your own heart and soul.

But do you know what most people mistakenly do? They worship the symbol and get all involved in protecting the symbol. They worship the metaphor instead of reality and then defend their metaphors among one another. "I have the true metaphor." And then we worship ourselves holding these "true" metaphors and images. You know what that's called? Idolatry. Idolatry means to worship not God but the image of God. Much religion is in direct violation of the very first commandment.

The Way of Asceticism. The path of asceticism can also be very dangerous. The danger is that this path of discipline, taking the hard way, can lead you to thinking that hardship and difficulty of themselves will bring you to God. Jesus certainly did not walk the way of asceticism. Jesus always dismisses any kind of dietary rigor. He never says, "Don't eat this, don't do that." Religious leaders of his day made fun of him because he was not like John the Baptist; he didn't go out into the desert and take the hard way. Hardness of itself does not please God. The Buddha also passed through the way of the ascetic but eventually rejected it.

The Way of Secret Wisdom. There is a path that journeys through the psyche. It's very common today. We used to call it "gnosticism." It's also recognized as the way of arcane knowledge, the way of the shaman, the way of the wise woman. In this path, the person goes inside to attain secret wisdom. If you want to see this path in action, just take a trip to Santa Fe. Our state of New Mexico glories in ways of secret wisdom. It's a genuine path, but it also has its dangers, because it keeps religion highly localized in the private head. But it's a path. Stay on it and keep learning, until it leads you to incarnation, commitment, and what Annie Dillard calls "the scandal of particularity." FIVEs need to go on this path.

The Way of the Laborer. There's the path of labor — no particular kind of labor, just hard work with your hands. We celebrate the feast of St. Joseph the Worker on May 1. Work was apparently Joseph's path.

My father grew up on a farm and worked for the railroad thirty-five years and never missed a day of work. When he listens to my cassette programs, he says to me, "Where do you get all those ideas? I never taught you that." My father is a simple man. He didn't finish grade school. He labored all his life. Work, work, work.

But I observed his mellowness, his freedom, his ability to love us children and my mother all his life. He knew how to trust the poverty of things. He wouldn't harm a fly. He couldn't imagine killing anything. I think he's arrived at the preeminent path, though I suppose he'd never think so, nor would he know how to name it. He's just a laborer doing things with his hands. He doesn't think he's a mystic, doesn't think he's religious, doesn't think he's anything great or heroic. But he does know he's been faithful; he knows he's stayed on his path all the way through.

I had the privilege of preaching at my parents' fiftieth wedding anniversary. My mom and dad were sitting in the front with my brothers and sisters. I told the story of how we kids would crawl on his lap and play with his wedding ring. I pointed out that my dad never let us move the ring past his second knuckle. Picture me standing up in the big parish pulpit. Dad was sitting there and I was telling this story to the whole church. Then I looked at him and asked him, "Daddy, have you ever taken it past the second knuckle?"

He sort of cried a little, looked up at me, shook his head, and quietly said, "No, I never have."

That's faithfulness. That's the kind of loyalty that may seem silly to a lot of people today. But I know that in his simple way the statement "No, I never have" summed up everything he wanted to say. His life of labor and effort led him to his own kind of mysticism, his own unique kind of holiness.

The Way of Politics and Social Action. On the path of politics and social action people get engaged with this world. They listen to it, sense its pain, and get involved in the lessening of that pain. Their goal is to bring about truth and justice. Of itself, the path of politics and social action is not *the* path, but it can lead you to the path of littleness, the path of nonviolence.

The Path of Parenting. The path of parenting is one many are destined to follow. It involves raising their children and seeing their children through the triumphs and defeats of life. Parenting is clearly their path to holiness. They can't afford all the time needed for annual retreats that we religious enjoy; they may not get to read many spiritual books. But they raised their children, and that experience was their teacher and spiritual guide.

The Path of Science and Technology. On the path of science and technology people are involved in creating some new idea, principle, machine, or process that will give more freedom and life to this world. As we move about our daily life using telephones, televisions, computers, cars, airplanes, kitchen appliances, supermarkets, elevators, air conditioners, and all the rest, we all thank God people are on this path. Hopefully, like all paths, it will self-destruct by its own good will. It will lead us to the edge of what we know and drop us off into mystery and miracle.

•

These are just some representative paths. I could name dozens more ways people have made their journey to God successfully. And so could you.

Those on No Path

There are also many people, maybe even the majority if my observation is correct, who are on no path. Really, on no consistent path at all. To me, it would be the noonday devil of death to be randomly trying out this path for fun, tasting that one a bit, enjoying this one for a while, going to workshops here and there to experience this path and that. These are the folks who sample paths like hors d'oeuvres: a bite of religion, a nibble of art, a smidgen of asceticism, science, and work. To me, that's no path. That's not even living. It means such people do not understand the journey.

They can never write their own Canterbury Tale. Chaucer's medieval legend is saying the same thing I have been saying about following one's path. All the pilgrims journeying toward Canterbury are facing their own capital sin and their own darkness, and yet they are on their way to the place of the great temple.

To follow no clear and consistent path avoids going through the flow of the life and death of Christ. It avoids experiencing the *inferno*, the *purgatorio*, and the *paradiso*.

The Enneagram Paths

In Chapter 5, I present the nine Enneagram paths and show how they are also paths we can trust and listen to.

After you get to know each of the nine paths, you'll be ready to recognize the gift of your particular path. You'll recognize what is good about the passion/anger of a ONE, for example.

As you study your own special path, ask yourself: Where has it allowed me to go and what part of God have I been able to trust? What is the gift of my path and what has it allowed me to see and do?

But first you must understand how your center affects your conversion and spiritual transformation.

4

The Courage to Live

In spiritual practice, we are always trying to center ourselves and live at that place where we are who we truly are. Our desire is to be at home at that place of our initial, original creation, that center where God from the beginning said it was good. Most of us spend all of our lives trying to get back to that place. For some reason we never seem to feel at home there, yet we want to be at home there. We want to live out of our gift, out of that which is good in us, that which is very good.

You may recall that after each day of creation in the Genesis account, after God created planets, stars, sun and moon, and then humanity, the text says, "and it was very good" (Gen. 1:10–31). However, after each of the first two days of creation Scripture does not say, "it was very good." It omits that blessing or observation (Gen. 1:3–8).

The first exception was the day when light and darkness were separated. The second was when heaven and earth were separated. In both those cases, the text does not say, "it was very good."

Yet what was done on all the other days was very good. Why the difference?

Perhaps in a spiritual sense it was not good to separate either heaven and earth or light and darkness, because the fundamental task in the spiritual life is precisely to try to rejoin the unity that got separated. In our spiritual work, we are struggling to put together again heaven and earth, the sacred and the secular.

The disappointment so many of us in religious life have felt is that the monastery and the church kept the sacred and the secular separated. Thus, the real task of spirituality remains: to put them back together again. That's what we're working toward through the Enneagram.

I think it was C. S. Lewis who said, "The basic spiritual virtue is courage." The dominant theme of courage in M. Scott Peck's *The Road Less Traveled* is one reason why I'm sure it continues to speak deeply to people. That it stays on the bestseller lists year after year is a sign that people need a guide for the spiritual journey who understands their lack of courage. Scott Peck addresses the fact that we don't seem to have the courage to walk the spiritual journey. He gives us reasons for having that courage, and people like him for that.

Rollo May in his book *Man's Search for Himself* says that the most frightening step in the human journey is for us is to accept responsibility for our own path and our own judgments, especially when we know how limited and imperfect we are. Of course, one problem is many people don't know how limited and imperfect they are. Yet they accept responsibility for their choices and they go with them.

Blaise Pascal says, "You have no choice; you must place your bet."

Truly, you have no choice. You are alive. You are here. You are moving forward in time. You are on the journey. You have no choice but to be on it. You cannot *not* choose to be on it. Yet to place your bet on this path or that, to take some road less traveled, is an act of courage.

This, says Rollo May, is what Paul Tillich means by the courage to accept one's finiteness. Accepting that finiteness, May holds, is the basic courage every person must have. It is the courage to be and to trust yourself, despite the fact that you are finite. Courage means continuing to be loving, thinking, creating, and making choices, even though you know that you do not have the final answers. But still you go ahead with it.

Put those two together and it comes out: "I don't have the final answer, but I've still got to act."

Perhaps, from the Enneagram's perspective, we can now understand why we often remain in our paralysis and fear.

"What if I'm wrong?" The SIX worries.

"What if I'm not perfect?" the ONE asks.

"What if they won't love me?" the TWO wonders.

And so we can each find our excuses for our fear, "good reasons" why we don't act.

The challenge is to go on loving, thinking, creating, and making choices, even though we know we do not have the final answers.

And we may even be wrong.

Self-Giving

If the providence of God means anything to me, it means God giving me the freedom to be wrong. What else could God be doing in divine providence? Look at this planet! Look at our lives! God is allowing us again and again to be wrong and, out of our wrong choices, making life happen.

Where do we get this idea that we cannot be wrong? That the most important commandment is "Thou shall not be wrong"?

God's commandment is very clearly "Thou shall love." God's path is love. The path of loving is very different from the path of avoiding wrong.

The fuller commandment is: "You shall love the Lord your God with all your heart and soul; you shall love your neighbor as yourself." All three objects of our love are important: yourself, your neighbor, and God.

God's call is to stay on the path toward love.

Rollo May says the greatest block to our development of courage is our having to adopt *a way of life that is not rooted in our own powers.* So, many of us end up doing something that is not us. We are acting out of another agenda, following a path that is not our path.

For example, over the years I've met many people, women especially, who have taken on the TWO path, and they are clearly not TWOs. They suffer for it. Our culture tells them: "If you're a woman, you're supposed to be a servant who waits on your husband and children." Obediently they conclude, "Well, that's who I have to be or I'm not a good woman." And so they place their bets, they follow this path and they suffer. TWO is not who they really are; this is not their true self. Yet no one gives them the courage or the call to be themselves, to "go with it."

"You have no choice; you must place your bet."

I hope the Enneagram frees us all to place our bets on who we are, which is what God created us to be.

Isak Dinesen says:

I think that unless one is oneself one cannot do anything much for others. With the best will in the world, and even with a great deal of effort, one will always, to a certain extent, give them stones instead of bread. *And both sides know it.*

Unless one is true to oneself. I'm not talking about cheap individualism that says "I gotta be me, no matter what." No, I'm talking about reaching down to your initial creation, acknowledging it, and taking responsibility for it. Unless you are yourself, you cannot do anything much for others. In the end, it's really *yourself* that you give to others.

That's what I think is meant in the gospel when Jesus says he is giving us his flesh for the life of the world. He gives us himself. It's as though he says, "*Eat* me" as well as "Eat *me.*" Eating is a very physical action. Jesus doesn't give us primarily his ideas or his teaching but himself, his flesh. "Eat who I am."

Ultimately, all we can give one another is who we are. All we can share is the path we have been willing to walk. If you've been willing to take the risks, and let your SIXness or your FOURness unfold, you have a lot to give people. And what you finally give them is the process itself.

One of the readers of our little newsletter *Radical Grace* wrote a note to praise our publication. What she liked about the publication was that we didn't give readers conclusions and answers as much as we offered them a process, a way. We provided ways to listen, ways to let go, ways to hear.

All that is based on a trust that God is involved in everything we do. We at *Radical Grace* trust in providence, so we don't have to give you all the answers.

If you can move yourself out of the way in a complete act of trust, God will give you the truth. I don't need to convince believers of that. Those on the spiritual journey already know it.

Unfortunately, what we've done in the Christian tradition is turn the gospel into an ideology, a head trip, a philosophy and theology competing with other philosophies and ideologies.

Jesus doesn't walk around saying "believe this" or "believe that." Instead he says *"follow me"* through passion, death, and hopeful resurrection.

Rather, what we need to be affirming is God's providence in daily action. We need to be saying, "Yes, I can trust that the Holy Spirit is working with me, that God is in my life, that God is in my very creation. And I trust that creation is already moving toward redemption."

All you have to do is learn to trust the initial creation. Once you do that, process is much more important than conclusion.

When I talk to people, I try to give them myself. I know I've taken a certain kind of risk that sometimes I'm ashamed of in my lectures. As you know, I don't talk from prepared notes. Usually, I'll just have some scattered quotes in front of me, so I risk going off on tangents. I risk using poor sentence structure and bad English, as well as stuttering. And I risk confusing people for a while, but it's the only way I know to give people *myself.* My text may not be nearly as well prepared as others', and my ideas may not be as clearly presented, and in some ways I don't sound as professional. Nonetheless, I have a sense that in this way people see my vulnerability, my ordinariness, my anger, my judgments. I also hope they see some kind of humanity through it all.

And I'm speaking for all of us: We've all got to do the same for each other. We've got to give one another our flesh. Not just our ideas, advice, ideals, or our neatly packaged conclusions.

Robbing Our Energy

I suspect that when we are into our compulsiveness, which we all get into especially in times of stress, we find it unfamiliar and uncomfortable to act and choose in line with our "health."

Have you ever had someone stop you when you're in your compulsive flow? Don't you tend to resent them? In effect, you say, "I don't want to go back to health. It sort of feels nice here, in some perverse way."

For example, I was rushing around the house yesterday, trying to get a lot of things done before a public program. Dan, who had been a guest at our house the past few days, said, "Richard, slow down. Slow down. I don't think you're centered and you've got to talk tonight."

Inside myself, I could feel my angry reaction, "Oh, dammit! I'm not distracted. I'm running around precisely so that everything will be in place so I will be able to talk tonight."

But I didn't like being told that. I was comfortable in my unhealth! I wanted to turn back at him and shout, "I'm centered. Don't slow me down now." Ironically, we can always find good reasons for avoiding our health.

We can always find good reasons to stay in the compulsive flow, to stay in the groove we're in. And I want to underscore that tactic because we're all going to experience ourselves offering good reasons for the perverse things we do.

At times, people will catch us in our flow. When our sin is first pointed out, we will normally resent it, even when it comes from our friends. One nice thing about the Enneagram, though, is that these simple numbers provide a nonthreatening jargon for friends to challenge one another. We used Enneagram numbers a lot back in the community in Cincinnati. We'd say, "You're into your EIGHT." That's all it took.

But I warn you, when someone says, "You're into your EIGHT," or whatever number, don't be surprised that for at least thirty seconds you may not like that person. I tell you that ahead of time so you won't be surprised when it happens, and you won't take it out on the other person. None of us likes being caught in our compulsion. None of us likes that familiar flow being exposed or named. It's an embarrassment.

It's humiliating, especially because right at that moment it's the way you're getting your energy. You're getting your energy from your compulsion and they are daring to take it away from you. It feels like a kind of robbery — even a kind of stabbing, a kind of death. Certainly a kind of humiliation.

Three Styles of Leadership

Now, in looking at the Enneagram I'd like to emphasize as much as possible the Enneagram's gift — what is good about being the number we are.

Let me begin in a simple way with what I describe as three different styles of leadership. They correspond to the three Enneagram centers: Gut, Heart, and Head.

The Power Leaders. There are great variations within these centers. Nevertheless, I normally look on Gut people as the classic leader types. I call the EIGHTs, the NINEs, and the ONEs, each in their own way, the power leaders because they give movement and energy to things by their anger, by their zeal, by their passion, by their outspokenness, by their clarity, by their focus. What Gut people give to an event is movement and energy. You wouldn't think NINEs would provide dynamism in an event, but in their own unfocused way they do. Because they don't threaten any of us, we listen to them. They can speak in simple, clear statements that evoke our trust. They can be power leaders because they don't push us. But having only a power leader — a strong Gut person — is not enough to produce real change and real wholeness in people. What is also needed are relationship leaders and visionary leaders.

Relationship Leaders. The Head and Heart people are the ones who can really stir up the desire for change in people as well as the desire for wholeness. Often these Head people and Heart people don't look like leadership people who are creating the flow and the focus of a group or the direction of events, but I see it differently.

For example, I see Heart people, TWOs, THREEs, and FOURs, as relationship leaders. Their antennae are out picking up the energy of the group, sensing where the crowd is at, what people need, and where people are hurting. Unless that affective dimension is brought to an event, group, or institution, the power leadership of the EIGHT or the ONE may remain very ineffective and, in fact, even become destructive.

I think that's why we're talking increasingly in the church about collegiality, collegial leadership, team leadership, and partnership. We find ourselves mistrusting more and more the "one-man show," because one person alone does not provide enough breadth and depth of leadership, no matter who that one person might be. One person alone is not whole enough, not balanced enough. With only one person, you tend to get too much Gut, too much Head, or too much Heart.

You can see this imbalance often in a parish at a change of pastors. When the new pastor comes aboard, the whole parish must adjust to an entirely new leadership style. Perhaps for years they had a Gut person and now they have a Heart person. And that Heart person emphasizes a whole new set of concerns, approaches, procedures, and events the other person didn't. Personally, I think this is one reason why in our church the Lord is taking away the priesthood, apparently to force us into team leadership, into partnership, into collegiality. And ultimately we will recognize that we all have many gifts and that these gifts are better utilized when shared in union with one another.

Of course, teams and partnerships create a whole new set of problems. Any of you who have worked on teams know how difficult it can be. We have to spend much time having "check-ins" to make sure we're still present to each other, still together, still thinking as a team. In our community, we have Thursday morning "check-ins," which provide the only way we can share the feelings and anxieties that each of us is facing and feeling.

Visionary Leaders. The third Enneagram center is the Head. From among the Head people, we find visionary leadership. These are the ones who can perform leadership work that deals with information, with data, with perception, with the tradition a SIX might bring, the books a FIVE might have read, and the wonderful future a SEVEN might envision. That visioning energy of the Head broadens leadership and deepens it at the same time.

That's a very simplified overview of styles of leadership.

•

The Gut people are normally the power leaders, although THREEs can participate in power in their own way. But after all is said and done, I want you to remember that THREEs are Heart persons. Therefore, they are not exercising power as the Gut people do, but, more than we realize, THREEs are getting their cues from the crowd. In order to be successful and to be liked, they need to take their cues from others and read the response of the crowd. This can keep them from the movement and energy needed in a power leader. Heart people are really taking the temperature of the crowd and polling the crowd in order to name what the people want. We Americans have seen this in Ronald Reagan and Bill Clinton, with different results.

Watching for these cues, while it is their gift, can also be their entrapment and their weakness, because they so need to be successful in people's eyes and need to be liked by the people around them.

Even so, a redeemed THREE can be a marvelous leader. We see this in heads of a lot of businesses. When redeemed, THREEs can lead, they can organize, they can manage, they can put it together probably better than any of the rest of us.

Head People

Let me make a few generalizations about the differences among the Heart, Head, and Gut people from the perspective of prayer and in terms of inner and outer focus. Though these are only generalizations, there is a large truth in them, so try to recognize the truth that's there.

In general, Head people have a small outer world and a large inner world. They're much more comfortable going inside. That's where they go to work things out. That may sound surprising, for a SEVEN in particular, but there is actually a lot of computer work going on inside the head of a SEVEN.

A major difficulty for Head people is how to be and act in the outer world. SEVENs actually have a lot of anxiety about being in the outer world. That's why they're constantly trying to reframe the outer world, in order to make it beautiful and fun. Normally, these people don't see their anxiety; SEVENs have one of the best disguises around. You wouldn't think of SEVENs as anxious people. They are. There is a constant anxiety in the SEVEN that the world out there is going to cause them some pain. "How can I create a Disneyland so I can avoid the world in its anxious form?" For Head people, fear is their least-controlled emotion.

In each of the three Enneagram centers the middle number, the THREE, SIX, and NINE are the real, primal, archetypal numbers, while the other two are variations on that middle type. FIVE and SEVEN are variations on SIX's anxiety energy. Anxiety remains a quiet stream inside of each of the Head types.

To overcome this anxiety FIVEs run into their heads to collect information, to get the facts clearly in place.

In contrast, to overcome their anxiety SEVENs run into their heads to generate creations of fancy and fantasy.

It's very important that the SEVENs and FIVEs see that they also, in their disguised and hidden ways, are people of fear. Fear is why the dogmatism of FIVEs can become so laborious and so burdensome to everyone else. They're always coming to you suspicious about the new theology and "Have you noticed this dangerous tendency?" I get fear letters from FIVEs all the time — pages and pages of anxiety and fear. "Here are the dangers of liberation theology" and "Have you read this, Richard?" and "Better watch out for that."

Their search for knowledge is distorted and diverted by an unrecognized fear. Therefore, in prayer you need to help your Head move to a kind of focused meditation to get some clarity, to get some calmness. That core of anxiety is why the whole Buddhist and contemplative tradition is focused in the Head space. The apophatic tradition of letting go of the mind is the needed prayer form for Head people.

The task for Head people is to learn how to detach from anxiety, how to find your center and your clarity so that fear can be named and let go of, not be the emotional setting in which you work, and not be called something other than fear.

For example, Catholic FIVEs and SIXes often call their fear "loyalty to the pope." Protestant FIVEs and SIXes might say, "I'm being obedient to the authority of the Bible." Well, maybe what you say is true, but more likely it's that you're afraid. I suspect you don't care *that* much about the Bible or the pope. More likely, you want to make sure you're right, mentally safe and secure, so you'll find some quote from the pope or some quote from the Bible to guarantee you're on solid ground.

Head people are trying to integrate their overdeveloped inner world with an outer world where they are much less secure.

Heart People

Heart people — TWOs, THREEs, and FOURs — tend to have a small inner world and a large outer world where they put their focus. This is where they're getting all their cues, and their energy is coming from interacting with one another.

For example, the FOUR needs you looking at him and saying, "Wow, he looks classy. He looks like he stepped off the cover of GQ." I don't know what FOURs would do if they didn't have someone to admire them and think they were attractive. THREEs and FOURs both dress well, but it's a different kind of well-dressed; "cool-looking" is more the THREE's favorite compliment; "exotic" is more the FOUR's.

For Heart people, God is usually found in expressive forms of prayer, good, healthy affective prayer. Inner concern about whether others are in sync with them or they are in sync with others is merely another kind of anxiety. For Head people it's fear of not being right; for Heart people it's anxiety about relationships, a primal insecurity about their person.

Heart people seek those feelings of ecstasy, of desire, of warmth; they need to express them, name them, and claim them as their own. The psalms have many words and phrases that can speak deeply to Heart people, because the psalms are filled with expressive kinds of words that name the heart, give voice to that inner world, and show us how to link it with the outer world. That's why in prayer Heart people like poetry and music. They tend toward symbol and ritual. They need ways to get their small inner world expressed in the outer world.

To some extent, we all need that, and we all need to move out of our own space. We obviously need different liturgical prayer forms in the church and different spiritual life prayer forms in our own personal journey. One form is simply not enough for everybody.

For Head people, God is very much outer; they're always trying to comprehend this God out there, explain how God is working and who God is. But Head people simply have got to get answers to their questions. "What is the meaning of God?" You'll recognize Head people because they'll be looking for the correct name for God, the correct theology to believe in. And then they'll fight over what they have learned or discovered. Which theology is the correct one? Because they have a small outer world where they feel awkward and not very secure, they need a God-out-there who names and defines the outer world for them.

For Heart people, in contrast, God is very inner. God dwells within as a lover, as a presence, as a warm companion. They might say, "God is working within me, giving me energy, and walking with me." That's the God Heart people can best fall in love with, best trust, and best be able to move with.

Gut People

Now Gut people — EIGHTs, NINEs, and ONEs — move back and forth between the inner and the outer worlds. That's their strength and their weakness. They can be, at their best, equally developed — inner and outer, where they alternately live. When they're living in one, they can dissociate from the other, and that's when they can be very destructive.

That's why we Gut people are always wanting silence. You see it especially in ONEs, but I see it in healthy EIGHTs, too. They need to refind their center. We Gut people talk so much about getting centered because it is the only way we can creatively connect the inner and the outer worlds. Our needed prayer form is silence, nature, expanses of open space within and without.

I can see why I named our center, "The Center for Action and Contemplation." I'm solving my own problem! How do I live in both worlds? I've got to do both, and sometimes I don't know how to do both. But that's the issue with which a Gut person is involved.

For Heart people, their least-controlled emotion is insecurity about relatedness; it moves them to reconnect with people, in order to overcome that anxiety. We call them social types.

For Head people, their least-controlled emotion is fear; they are fear/flight people. As soon as they feel the fear, they flee from it. We call them self-preservative types.

For us Gut people, our least-controlled emotion is anger; we're anger/fight people. Instead of running away from fear as the Head people do, Gut people attack it head on. We call them aggressive types.

Gut people move into things with their anger, with their judgments, and with their passion. Even NINEs are attacking — but in a unique way, by being passively aggressive. The NINEs are always more of an exception anyway. Their approach to reality does not fit the common flow.

For the Gut person God is within and without. God is the one who connects the two worlds — the inner and outer. ONEs can be good teachers when they make those connections for you. And EIGHTs can be powerful leaders provided they make that same connection for the people.

I hear the inner-outer connection in the preaching of Jesse Jackson, for example. As an EIGHT, he's still a preacher even when he's talking like a politician. He's always talking about the soul — the inner life, values of the soul, and the things we do that really matter. That's how he thrills people and scares them at the same time; he's connecting their inner world and their outer worlds more than Americans want to have them connected.

As a rule, we don't want to connect our spirituality to our politics. "We don't like you for that, Jesse; we don't want to deal with someone like you." Martin Luther King had been doing the same thing, of course. That's the ability of the power leader — to be able to make that connection for us.

However, power leaders can be very destructive leaders, too, if they are not linking the two worlds. Some Gut people are totally into their outer world, which would be the more common failing. Others are totally into the inner world, much as we ONEs can get caught up in our legalistic principles.

A ONE who really hasn't grown up and has just learned a few laws or a few Bible quotes is going to lay his or her stuff on you. "This is the only way to do it" or "This is the only way to be saved" or "This is the only way to be right." Because these ONEs are coming from a place that is totally inner, their communication is wooden, rigid, and cold. Limited as they are, these Gut people can still be leaders.

In my opinion, many religious leaders in history have been very compulsive. That would certainly be the limitation of both Calvin and Luther. (I say that not from a Catholic perspective; Protestant friends have pointed this out to me.) Both Calvin and Luther were ONEs, unredeemed ONEs. They took their inner principles and got compulsively angry over them. There was too much moralizing, too much judgment, too much focus. It was all inner focus and they provided no connection with the outer world.

With either of them, it was difficult to find any major concern with the Sermon on the Mount, for example, for what we call the corporal works of mercy, the ministry of social justice. Their theology was almost all "inner" salvation theories as well as behavioral theories that they imposed on people. This is what happens when ONEs do not make the connection between their "inner gut" and their "outer gut" response to reality.

Gut people, therefore, must have *space* around their ideas, their opinions, their feelings, their relationships. Any prayer form that provides them with "holy spaciousness" will allow them to hold on to things less tightly, to be loose around their driven ego, and to have room for the other. Thus they often resist overstructured, ververbal, and overdrawn prayer styles.

5

The Nine Enneagram Paths

Here I want to describe what I mean by the nine paths of the Enneagram. I believe that each of these nine paths has the potential to lead us to the preeminent path of Jesus. His is the path of universal love and nonviolence toward all, the path that leads us to trust that which is broken, poor, and little — the poverty and universal love of Jesus.

These nine Enneagram paths help us to solve our own personal problems, but I think our own churches and our own denominations need help from the Enneagram as well. In our churches we've been told we're on the Jesus path. Sometimes, perhaps, religion and church and sacraments and Bible do lead people to the Jesus path. However, when we're really honest about things, we have to admit that much of what goes on in our churches has nothing to do with the Jesus path. Things never seem to get there.

Instead churches offer the path of religion, or the path of pseudo-mysticism, or the path of righteousness, or some other road. I'm not saying those paths are wrong. I hope each road will get people to the Jesus path someday. However, in my own mind, I need to make a distinction between what churches profess to offer and what they in fact do. From my perspective, much of institutional religion has nothing to do with the Jesus path.

It is amazing that so called orthodoxy is usually "orthodox" in only a few self-chosen areas, usually having to do with questions of power or authority and questions of body or sexuality... looks very suspicious to me! Leadership with such a focus can go on for millennia and never worry about the Sermon on the Mount — never even quote the Sermon on the Mount.

That sermon outlines the quintessential Jesus path. There Jesus is saying, "Love your enemies, turn the other cheek, powerlessness is a new kind of power, be nonviolent." That teaching is so radical, so refined, and so purified that much of institutional religion has simply not been ready for it and has avoided it; instead, it has taken other minutiae — insignificant rules and regulations — around the corners of the Sermon and then become dogmatic about them. Probably an effective avoidance.

But I don't get into my ONE anger over it anymore. It's okay for people to be on the religion path. I hope it leads them to the Jesus path. I'm not there yet. I hope I get there someday. And I hope these nine paths can provide a way to lead us all there.

I hope you like the names I chose for the nine paths. I worked on them. I wanted to make them positive, and I think they're honest.

ONE: The Path of Desire

I call Enneagram number ONE the path of desire — desire for things as they should be. It's a focused desire that we cannot, for some reason, let go of. It's an archetypal energy that's wired into our soul that, by midlife, begins to burden us. We wish we could let go of it, cut the wires. But it overpowers us; it grabs us with its teeth like a bulldog. It's there almost every moment. It leads us to be dissatisfied with things as they are, because our desire for things as they should be is so strong. We don't know how not to desire things to be as they should be. We are preoccupied with what ought to be. That is the path of desire.

And desire is good. In fact, if as a ONE you do not feel such strong desire, if you are not filled with desire, then pray for the gift of desire. You *must* desire, because what you desire is what you will become. What will happen to you is what you finally deeply desire. Desire is a gift of the Spirit.

It's a shame we tend to associate desire with something negative or exclusively sexual, when it is clearly the passion and the power of God within us creating movement and energy toward what can be. Remember, that's the Gut movement — movement and energy toward. Without Gut people there's not going to be much movement or energy into the future, or toward anything. Let your desire be toward a big vision or call.

So I want ONEs to trust that desire, to taste it, to observe it, to hold that desire. Identify the best part of it, the part that is really leading you to the values of what we call in Christianity "the kingdom," which embodies the universal values of unity, goodness, truth, and beauty.

The reason I encourage this expansion of desire is because, normally, our desires are trapped within a small egocentric world: "I want things this way."

Egocentric desire is a petty, whiny thing. Some examples of little desires might be: "I like things on time" or "I want my food prepared just this way" or "I want the table kept clean." Well, that's fine, ONEs, but your clean house really doesn't have much to do with the kingdom. It's merely what you want. I'm picking on myself here, as you know, since I'm a ONE.

"Who cares if your house is clean?"

I do!

But I've got to discriminate in my desires. I've got to look closely at this desire for cleanliness and observe, "Now, this clean house is much more my mother inside of me — and now me — and it's really not an ultimate value of the kingdom."

But even when I say this to myself, there's still that tug, that pull that creates momentary dissatisfaction and discomfort when the house is dirty — or whatever else happens to be keeping my personal world from being perfect, beautiful, and right.

A ONE during crisis or under stress will invariably be trying to clean up something. Just to get my vacuum cleaner out and run it through the house makes me feel good. It's so stupid, and I recognize what I'm doing, but I still do it. It's part of being a ONE.

At the Center they see me running around emptying wastebaskets. They know what I'm up to. "He's into it now," they say to one another. "He's angry about something." I cannot seem to do otherwise. The church or the world has become so overwhelming to me — warfare or drug trafficking or crime on the streets or whatever is making me angry, and I can't change the president and I can't change the pope — so I empty the wastebasket! And I say to myself, "I'm going to clean up this kitchen. At least this kitchen will be perfect. And it will make me feel good!"

In fact, I do feel better after this kitchen is clean. The church is still dirty and America is still dirty, but the kitchen is clean.

So this path of desire has to trust its focus. Our ONE focus is fundamentally good, but we've got to work for freedom in that focus. Our desire has got to be free from those petty egocentric concerns. It's got to be free for the bigger picture, the bigger truth. Ultimately the focus needs to be on the kingdom. That takes major courage. It takes a major conversion in a ONE to free that focus for the big picture.

The ONEs' focus on desire is our best gift; it's what people like about us. I've mentioned that I have more FOURs come to me for spiritual direction than any other Enneagram number. Somehow, FOURs always recognize that we ONEs are and have what they need: focus and clarity.

Those realizations reinforce my trust in the truth and value of the Enneagram, for example, when I see how many FOURs come to me for spiritual direction. FOURs don't have a lot of focus. NINEs don't either, but ONEs are too close to NINEs. On the other hand, FOURs are into their moods; they have sensitivity all over the place; and they want to know where to put it. They see ONEs having the clarity and the focus to know where to put it. Knowing how to do that is our gift.

But I want to tell you how that ability to focus is also our fault. We're so focused that it's easy to trigger our anger. For example, if you want to get me irritated, it's easy. If I'm talking to someone else, just stand right here next to me demanding my attention. This happens at every conference I attend. One person is saying to me, "I want you, I want your attention" while I'm trying to talk to another person. Do you see what happens to a ONE like me in this situation? My focus is split at this point, and I don't like that. I start getting angry inside. In my mind, I view this new person as an intruder and I am wishing, "Will you move away? I cannot be attentive to this person and you at the same time!"

People who work with me at the Center know this about me. It must be hard for them when I'm into my ONE focus and they want to talk to me about something else. It usually takes me thirty seconds or a minute to switch focus. I can't do it instantly.

I'm just pointing out how the gift for focus is also a ONE's liability. You resent it when someone forces a change of attention upon you and you don't know how to switch. So the path of desire, which keeps us ONEs going and moving forward, is also a liability, because somehow we don't know how to let go of that focus easily, even when an important interruption occurs.

People at our Center often tell me, "The interruptions are what we're all about." Now, I love that idea on paper. And some people at the Center are really good at dealing with interruptions. Someone can call them and they can let go of their present focus and give themselves to the moment, to the interruption. But it's hard for me to do that.

When I'm into something, I'm into it. This is one of my real personality weaknesses. I've worked on it for years and I still don't know how easily to switch that focus. I say that to free you, too, when you recognize that tendency inside yourself. It is hard for many of us ONEs to switch loves and to shift energies and desires.

TWO: The Path of Relationship

TWOs are on the path of relationship. Of all the paths, I believe this one is both the most wonderful and the most terrible, the most trustworthy and the most difficult. I also think it is the path on which God has called most of us to walk. It's probably why the majority of people are called to marriage, that is, to remain in one

relationship for the long term and to live through the agony and
ecstasy of one other person.

If we in Christianity believe that God *is* relationship — we call that
relationship "Trinity" — then the foundation of reality has to be love
and relatedness. And the foundational energy for relationship is the
capacity for giving and for receiving.

In Catholic theology, we express that loving relationship in a
highly sophisticated metaphor called "Father, Son, and Holy Spirit."
We're the only religion in the world that believes that God is
relationship.

For us, God is perfect giving and perfect receiving. We live our
lives in that sharing flow of love: the love of the Creator/Father
flowing in us and through us; the love of the Redeemer/Son who
receives the call to be a beloved and who, as Christ, reflects the Father's love back like a mirror. "Holy Spirit" is the name we give to
the Father-Son relationship. The Holy Spirit precisely *is* that relationship. In Catholic theology, the Spirit is defined or identified as
the "relationship between the Father and the Son." Thus, there are
three realities in God: the Creator/Father, the Redeemer/Son, and
the Spirit/Relationship between them.

And we the believers are the body of Christ. We are a part of that
divine love-flow, receiving it not only directly from the Creator but
also from the Redeemer/Son. That's what we mean by immanent,
incarnational Christianity. God is within.

"In" — that's the whole meaning of Christ. Without Christ, without us being the body of Christ, we don't have God here within us
and among us. We have only God totally transcendent. The Trinity
integrates the transcendence and immanence of God. So to live in
the Spirit is to live in that flow of divine relationship with all that
it offers you.

What it offers you is the paschal mystery of agony and ecstasy,
light and darkness.

A friend, a companion, a partner, is a mirror who will show
you your greatest and deepest beauty as well as your greatest and
deepest sin.

TWOs have to work for an enlightened love. This is a love that is
growing less and less attached to their own need for power, prestige,
and identity.

Attachment to power and prestige can be very humiliating for
Heart people to recognize and admit. Many of their attachments,
their co-dependencies, are quite obviously used for their own purposes. You see it most strongly in TWOs. They attach themselves,
link themselves, and connect themselves to other people saying,
"You give me my energy, my identity, my importance, my secu-

rity." By themselves, TWOs don't know who they are. They are not centered in themselves.

This is why it is so important, yet difficult, for TWOs, THREEs, and FOURs to go into contemplative prayer. They need to go into that centered prayer where they find their autonomy, their ground, their center. They must learn to find their center in themselves.

To enlighten the path of relationship you have to cut off relationship for a while, live without it. You have to find your own ground, your own identity, so that when you enter relationship again the relationship is not two people leaning on one another, but two people clearly standing alone, then coming together out of freedom, then moving forward together side by side, hopefully in the same direction. How many marriages do you know like that?

Usually in marriage, enlightened relationship happens later on because most people marry too young, before they've found their ground. That's all right, since most of the Enneagram paths run backward as well as forward. Not much of this enlightenment work follows sequentially. Sooner or later you have to find your own ground and identity; it is harder to do later, however, because you are imprinted and patterned by years of routine.

Unless TWOs can break their attachments, which usually means dealing with co-dependency, their lives will normally not become enlightened. The reason is because TWO energy is usually too needy, too cloying, too manipulative, too preoccupied with its own voice and the feedback it gets from others, and too devastated by nonsupport and nonlove.

But the gift TWOs bring is that charming capacity for vulnerability, for wearing their hearts on their sleeves. TWOs know how to share their souls, to share the language of the inner world and the heart with the rest of us. They create poetry, write love words, and speak sweet nothings, because that's the domain they understand and that's where they need to lead the rest of us. In their world the language of the heart is spoken, the language of relationship, of vulnerability, of caring, of sympathy and empathy, and also of cheap sentimentality.

I can often pick out TWOs simply by the overtones in their voices. Men always fall in love with the Center for Action and Contemplation when our TWO receptionist answers the phone! They want to meet this woman. When you're talking to her on the phone, her voice exudes warmth and welcome. Before you comprehend her words, her voice has already invited you here, it has already convinced you, "The world at our Center is very nice." You feel seduced — and I mean this in the best possible sense. A TWO is always on the make, not sexually, but for your soul.

So are THREEs and FOURs — they're on the make for your soul, too. They're pulling you in, seducing you to the world of the soul, where love and relationships can be trusted.

Without the vulnerability of the TWOs, we'll never be ready for our passionate and relational God. Without them, we would not know how to be involved in a loving, caring relationship with God. Without this enlightened TWO energy, religion quickly turns cold, abstract and theological.

Relationship is the path for orthodox Judaeo-Christianity. In these traditions, we're in relationship with a personal God. For us, God is not just an impersonal inner force. That's New Age doctrine, not Christianity. Christianity says God is a Person and we are in a passionate, desiring relatedness (there's the ONE and the TWO) with that Person.

At the same time, God is out after us as the Hound of Heaven. This metaphor of God in pursuit of us, "on the make," as it were, reflects the understanding of divine providence I mentioned earlier.

God is on the make for you more than you're on the make for God. All you have to do is be vulnerable and you'll get caught by God. You'll be made, you'll be loved, you'll be seduced and taken.

What would we do without TWO language? Life would have no sweetness to it. Without the Heart people, life would be all duty, responsibility, and power and no "leading strings of love," as Hosea says (Hos. 11:4). Strings, unfortunately, can both bind you together and bind you up. TWOs are good at both.

THREE: The Path of Work

I call Enneagram number THREE the path of work. THREEs are not afraid to do tasks, take on projects, organize groups and events, put things together and make them happen. The world would be a pretty fluffy, namby-pamby place without THREEs. The rest of us would sit around and hold hands or create big theories and have gut responses, but we wouldn't do anything with them to benefit the world. Redeemed THREEs are for creating the City of God, creating a new humanity that matters, putting together what works for the good of the planet.

How empty and bland would this century have been if we Americans hadn't brought some of our THREE energy to the world? That THREE energy brought technology, science, and industry together and created serums and vaccines that have healed people. THREE energy says: "I'm going to make it happen. Let's not just talk about things, let's not just feel things, let's make them happen."

THREEs love it when they can have at least ten irons in the fire at the same time. The rest of us envy them. "How can they do it?" we wonder.

For example, we ONEs want to preserve our focus: we want to do one thing well. I'm always saying this to the staff: "I don't care if the Center for Action and Contemplation has done a bunch of things. At the end, I'd like to be able to say we've done one or two things well. So we can't do all these other things."

But a THREE wants to do fifteen things well. However, normally, no one can do fifteen things well, so what they sacrifice is depth and thoroughness. In their action, they often, of necessity, have to settle for a certain level of superficiality. And that's what we name as their deceit: superficiality. Those fifteen irons in the fire may all come out half-baked. THREEs may seem to be doing them all coolly, smoothly, and easily, but normally THREEs won't ask the philosophical questions. They won't ask the important historical or moral questions behind what they're doing. If it works, it's true. If it works, it must be good.

Although their superficiality may be deceitful, at the same time, their path of work is a gift to all of us. This is easy to see when you compare it to the FIVE, who obsesses over metaphysical questions and seldom gets anything done. There has to be someone — thank God for the THREEs — to put the show on the road, to make something happen.

THREEs will say, "Okay, we've talked enough. You've brought your hearts and your heads to the project. What are we now going to do about it? When will we begin to take action?"

It is important that someone is free to pose that challenge. Really, very little good would have happened on this earth without THREEs, I'm convinced. Neither of the organizations that I supposedly founded in Cincinnati and here in Albuquerque would have gotten off the ground, except for a THREE at my side who made it happen in both cases. I don't know how to organize anything. All I do is stand up in front of a group and talk, and then I walk away. The people who work with me know me. They'll tell you, "He just talks, that's all. He doesn't know how to manage or organize anything or put anything together." In fact, at a recent workshop I had to ask one of my assistants how to organize the small discussion groups.

The important thing for THREEs to learn is to ensure that their work has truth to it and integrity. They often need help in this. But because they are Heart people, they can use their gift of relationship to make the necessary connections, especially the connections that will help them achieve depth. That's why, in their spiritual life, they have to set aside time for solitude. They must get in touch with their own center.

THREEs will normally admit to you that silence is terrifying. They operate in the middle of the Heart space. To ask them to go it alone in prayer for one hour is to cut off their energy flow, to cramp the style by which they motivate themselves. They're not going to know how to motivate themselves for an hour in contemplative prayer. And that's precisely why they have to do it — for enlightenment.

Only inner work and appropriate reading can provide the necessary depth and ground to their marvelous managerial skills. THREEs who have both energy and depth are highly effective persons. "Effective" is the best word you can use for a THREE.

But they have to seek truth, integrity, and depth. They need to learn to be contented with doing a few things thoroughly, instead of wanting always to do more. This involves a kind of letting go of excessive ambition, an excessive need to do more.

THREE energy sometimes almost looks like SEVEN energy, that is, "more is better." That's when THREEs are on their conveyor belt, when they are whipping the whole thing together and feeling tremendous energy in attacking seventeen projects before it's time to go to bed.

At such times, THREEs should pray for the gift of contentment. As the psalmist says, "content as a child weaned on its mother's lap" (Ps. 131:2).

My advice to the busy THREE is, "This moment is already full. This moment is rich. Go inside to discover the truth of what I say. Then bring that richness and insideness to the world of work. By the way, you need never apologize for the world of work or the path of work. Martha, "busy about many things," is also called Saint Martha. Her "lesser part" is still *a part!*

FOUR: The Path of Beauty

FOURs follow the path of beauty. Dostoyevsky speaks for them: "The world will be saved by beauty." FOURs love whatever is beautiful. They have an eye for beauty; when they see it, their heart delights in it. And then they suffer a bit, because the world is not as beautiful as their imaginings — or as they know it could be. They share in some way the desire of the ONE, but the FOUR's is an *aesthetic* desire, while the ONE's is an *idealistic* desire.

FOURs know what beauty can be and they must sit uncomfortably in ugly and tawdry churches. "How can I pray here!?" they cry. To FOURs, ambiance is very important. They love inner decor and tell me that even mediocre food can taste fine if the restaurant feels classy.

The temptation of a FOUR is to overdo it. You'll see an over-adorned FOUR wearing scarves, earrings, and jewelry, clashing colors and a bizarre outfit with outlandish shoes over Purple Monster socks. To that FOUR we say, "It's just too much. You've lost it. Not good taste. I know you're seeking beauty but what you've done is not beauty anymore." Many FOURs settle for eccentricity.

What FOURs have to work toward is an unadorned beauty: finding greatness in simplicity. Such spare, simple beauty you see in Japan. You see it in Zen spirituality or haiku poetry — that refined FOUR energy. They don't overdo it.

The FIVE wing of FOURs encourages them to focus on one tasteful thing: to seek beauty in the ordinary, in the simple.

Find just one tree, just look at this one tree. See how lovely it is, how beautiful it is. You don't have to dress up the tree. That's the kind of tasteful simplicity you'll see in a mature FOUR.

If you've ever been to a Zen temple, you know the experience of finding beauty in simplicity. I remember going up a mountain in Japan, walking from garden to garden, each arrangement becoming more simple as you ascended the mountain. At the top was a beautifully simple, perfectly formed thatched hut. When you opened its big wooden doors what you saw inside was a single spotlessly polished mirror in which you could see your face. It's been there since the fourteenth century. One man is assigned to polish it. The end result is this perfect clarity of form.

The Japanese culture, more than any culture I know, has achieved the perfection of the FOUR. FOURness has been emblazoned in its culture. Even though many Japanese have become THREEs now, they used to be FOURs. Even though they've moved over into their THREE wing, they've still got that leftover FOUR there, which is why they're beating the pants off of us in quality and style.

In contrast, America is a THREE with a TWO wing. When I was in Europe, a German said to me, "Americans always want to know if you love them. They are always asking us, 'Do you like America?' " Moreover, we're rather flashy THREEs, so we want everybody in the whole world to like us! Japanese THREEs don't have a great concern about being liked and approved because they're THREEs with a FOUR wing.

They move toward taste and class. Look at a Japanese product. Just the way it's wrapped reveals a tastefulness and class that America just doesn't have.

The second task for FOURs is to be contributing. They need to use their beauty and specialness, not just for their own narcissistic "My, don't I look good," but for the world. What the FOUR possesses must finally become a gift for others.

As a young woman, Martha Graham was a wonderful dancer, undoubtedly a redeemed FOUR, because the whole second half of her life was dedicated to making other young people great and beautiful dancers. That's the generosity you often see in a redeemed FOUR. They are always asking, "How can I make a contribution to the world, to bring out the specialness of others, instead of just my specialness?"

A redeemed FOUR is beautiful to see. You see it in Dan Berrigan asking, "How can I use this poetic gift for the cause of peace and justice?" He dedicates his literature to naming the elements of the cause, to ferreting out the false specialness, to displaying the real specialness, our dignity as creatures of God. You don't have to dress that up.

Like TWOs and THREEs, FOURs need contemplation. They can be very good at it because they have that FIVE wing. Nevertheless, they need to go inside and find their center. When they do, they discover that the unadorned truth is the greatest truth of all. They learn that the place of *nada*, of nothingness, is the place where everything resides, because it is the most spacious place of all. It is no surprise that Thomas Merton was a FOUR with a highly and beautifully developed FIVE wing.

If you look at the Enneagram diagram, you notice that the greatest space lies between the FOUR and the FIVE. If you can bridge that gap, you have a chance to become a most whole and effective person. Bridging the FOUR and FIVE means you are uniting the head and the heart. A healthy FOUR with a well-developed FIVE wing is normally a very effective person.

The reason Thomas Merton's writings captivate almost all of us, people of any religion, is because every paragraph challenges your head (because it's meaty intellectual stuff) and at the same time it's massaging your heart (because it's aesthetically beautiful and caring). You're just drawn into the truth and beauty of his writing.

The same would be true for FIVEs who have developed their FOUR wing, research scholars who can gather for the sake of communication and art, like James Michener. Most of us usually have to dig a tunnel between our head and our heart to allow them to inform one another indirectly.

FIVE: The Path of Knowledge

FIVEs tread the path of knowledge. The cognitive mind is what they're about. Of all the Enneagram numbers, FIVEs express most clearly the gift of intellect, which philosophers have always said differentiates us from the animal world.

Thomas Aquinas said that intellect and will were the primary human faculties. The Dominican tradition emphasizes intellect; the Franciscan tradition emphasizes will. Both are faculties that make us supremely human. FIVEs understand the gift of mind, of healthy thinking, grounded wisdom.

The key to the health of FIVEs is that they must move toward engagement. They must move toward involvement, commitment, specificity. Otherwise, they drift into abstract metaphysical thinking.

Just go to a metaphysical bookstore. You'll see shelves of unaccountable FIVE authors who've never grounded their thinking in tradition or other forms of knowledge. Unaccountable FIVEs drift into their own ozone trips, generating all kinds of theories, theologies, and abstractions. "Where am I being led? What does this mean?" is the feeling you get when you read their stuff. "What does this have to do with what anybody else has said?" FIVEs can live in an unreal world of their own making.

A lot of FIVEs may not have the discipline to write books, but they will spin yarns in a torrent of words. After listening a while to a FIVE talking, you'll say, "Do I need to hear this?" Talkative FIVEs go on and on spewing facts, information, and theories.

Other FIVEs don't talk very much, but when they do they can bore you to death with the details.

Their gift is found when they move toward specificity and concreteness and the passion of engagement. The task of the FIVE is to become an expert in *a few* things, and then use them to help others or our planet. We need their ability for disciplined specialization, although we too often get merely their theories and their mental avoidances.

Maybe it's mollusks and snails that fascinate you. Great. Learn all you can about those creatures and maybe you can help save us from impending ecological disaster. Move toward that kind of well-researched truth and let yourself feel your identity with the world and your caring for the world.

Sartre and Camus, two French existentialist philosophers, were both FIVEs. The last book they each wrote was on the same topic, the necessity of commitment. Eventually, FIVEs must stop merely thinking and start committing themselves to some concrete issue, cause, or person.

When they do, they become Jonas Salk and invent a vaccine that will heal polio. Thank you, Jonas, for using your FIVE energy to help the world instead of just spinning yarns. We need the love of objectivity, the love of fact and figure and directed research that only FIVEs have the patience to produce.

SIX: The Path of Loyalty

The SIX follows the path of loyalty. I believe with all my heart that SIXes are holding together most of the institutions of this world. I like to call them the "salt of the earth" people. They're the glue that's connecting everything. While the rest of us are running for the doors, they've got their feet firmly on the ground.

At a recent evening conference, I told the participants to talk in the breakout rooms until 9:30. Precisely at 9:30, the SIXes stood up and exited from their rooms because Father told them to talk until 9:30! God bless 'em. SIXes feel a loyalty to "what should be." The rest of us tend to skim over the rules or ignore them. In that sense, SIXes are very easy to work with. They hold the ground down, keep the building together, so there's something solid for the rest of us to plug into.

Our Franciscan province just elected a wonderful provincial and vice-provincial. I'm convinced they're both very healthy SIXes. During this rocky period, when religious life is unraveling all around us and everybody has one hand on the door, asking, "Do I want to get out before it all falls apart?" these SIXes will go down with the ship. I'm so grateful for their loyalty I want to hug them.

Within that loyalty, there's a humility about SIXes that the rest of us don't have. Their loyalty is to what is. Instead of running off into the sunset, flying off into ideals, or dropping off into the heart, SIXes are here present. They just humbly say, "This is it."

There's a man now working as a volunteer at our Center who quit his job at Sandia Labs, after his conscience told him he couldn't spend his life building weapons. Once SIXes come to their own truth, they're loyal to that truth, and they're going to let it lead them wherever it will. This man quit a well-paying job, and now he's answering mail at our Center for Action and Contemplation. For nothing. And he's always there on time. Loyal. He does whatever needs to be done. He doesn't care what it is, as long as it's needed. A healthy and productive SIX!

SIXes don't need to be front men. In fact, they prefer not to be. They merely ask, "How can I loyally help and support what I believe in?" They're great people. They'll stick with you forever. All you need to do is get a SIX loyal to a worthy cause.

The trouble is, many SIXes are into survivalism and the Ku Klux Klan. They end up being loyal to stupidity. That's why I say it's so important that SIXes, with their FIVE wings, bring some intelligence to their loyalty. I encourage SIXes to read serious books, to learn about history and politics, society and theology.

If you have an intelligent SIX on your team, you have a great person. They know what's worth being loyal to. And they are co-operative instead of just digging in their heels to protect themselves, develop conspiracy theories, or write paranoid letters to archbishops about the occult nature of the Enneagram!

SIXes are excellent partners. If you're married to a healthy SIX, you're going to have a loving, loyal marriage. As long as they don't abdicate their intelligence and become dogmatic, they'll stick with you and they'll stick with truth.

SEVEN: The Path of Joy

SEVENs are clearly on the path of joy. What they need to work toward is the refinement of that joy. They do this by incorporating pain, by going through the dark side and incorporating what hasn't worked. They need to work toward proportionality so their joy is not an overstatement but an honest response to the delight the occasion deserves. Often you feel they are overdoing it, excessively or falsely leading you into joy.

But at the same time, joy is their pure gift. SEVENs can always see what's good about things. They can see what is right and take delight in it, really take delight in it.

It took me a long time to recognize my father as a SEVEN, I guess because I'm so close to him. It's so obvious, looking back through my life, to see how Daddy could get a grin on his face about some small thing going well or something working out, while all the rest of the family would be frenetic and upset. He'd find the humor in it and he'd try to tease it out of my mother, who's an EIGHT and clearly couldn't find it. He had his optimist humor to put up with her passion. He would walk alongside her and make the best of it.

SEVENs are the people who know how to make the best of it. God knows, we ONEs can't do it; we make the worst of it. We see what's wrong; the SEVENs see what is right. While they have that half-smile on their face, the rest of us are terribly jealous of them, because they took ten years younger than they really are. It just doesn't seem fair. They keep their youth to an amazing degree.

So to the SEVENs I say, "Trust your happiness. Just refine it and temper it, unless you play the trumpet; then let it all burst forth in clarion ecstasy. Trust your optimism; the world needs it. Right now, we need your gift of hope, but we need a hope that is solid and well grounded, a hope that can still say, 'The world is good, this is God's world, and it is still God's church.'"

SEVENs are resurrection people; it's written in their creation. It's written in their bones. They are like Jesus at the wedding feast of Cana, who visited people in their gladness and intensified it further by multiplying the intoxication — a rather undeveloped Jesus-image but a very necessary one. SEVENs give us play and "dis-play," preparing us all to recognize the resurrection.

EIGHT: The Path of Power

EIGHTs clearly stride along the path of power. I debated about calling this the path of fearlessness, but it sounded rather negative, although it might fit better than power. However, power is not wrong. *Dynamis*, the Greek word for power, is the term that describes the Holy Spirit, so power cannot be inherently wrong.

Spirituality in an EIGHT usually supports a strong identification with masculine energy — in men or in women. The masculine archetypes are not mainly about separating men from women, but are all about how persons, male or female, handle power, how they integrate power, how they learn to trust their power. The task of EIGHTs is to discover why power is good, because the false feminine in men or women is always mistrustful of power.

Liberals, as a rule, are very mistrustful of power, whereas conservatives are mistrustful of powerlessness. What EIGHTs are saying to all of us is that power is good, and we're going to show you how to use power well in order to change things.

If anybody gives energy and movement to reality and to this world, it's EIGHTs. Without them, many things would never change. There would be no revolutions. There would be no one strong enough to stand up to the dictators and the stupid people of this world.

EIGHTs are against injustice. God created a certain set of people who simply don't care what you think about them and who actually take a certain delight in your hating them, a certain glee in your thinking they're terrible.

Thank God there are some EIGHTs who are not afraid to say, even to God's people, "You sonsabitches, stop doing that! How dare you oppress God's people! How dare you destroy God's creation! To make sure you stop, I'm going to stand in your way."

That's the unadulterated courage EIGHTs can bring to an unjust situation.

But like all of us, they must learn to detach themselves from their own egocentricity. They must learn to stop themselves when they discover they're playing the power game for the sake of their own power.

Saddam Hussein is clearly a sick EIGHT. George Bush, a counterphobic SIX, played his cards utterly wrong. You could say we went to war in the Persian Gulf so George Bush could prove he was not a wimp, so he could prove he is not a SIX, which he clearly is. Once he tried to stand up to Saddam Hussein and started sending troops over there, Saddam stood even stronger. When you start attacking EIGHTs, they stand up taller and taller.

If we as a people were much more savvy about the inner world, we wouldn't make these horrible political mistakes. Once you understand the Enneagram, for example, you quickly realize you never have a chance of winning with EIGHTs if you start yelling. They will always yell louder than you. They will always win.

What EIGHTs must get in touch with is their own nurturing center. EIGHTs, you must use your power for caring.

My mother was an EIGHT. She was a marvelous mother, an outstanding, nurturing mother — as long as we were babies. We couldn't have asked for more attention, more hugs, more kissing and caring. When we were sick, she was there next to us all night long. If we had to go to the hospital, she never left the hospital until we did. "I'm there for my kids, 150 percent" was her motto. As a result, all four of us children are very secure in that sense. We got good mothering. We had an EIGHT mother who knew how to bring that EIGHT passion to nurturance. "Tiger mothers" they call them.

Once we grew to be six and seven years old and started getting minds of our own, it was different. We began to feel our own power coming up against Mom's power, which created a totally different scenario.

EIGHTs know how to nurture, to bring power for caring, for the world, for the planet, but they must be passionate about specific people. Far too often, they are passionate about being passionate, passionate about *their idea* of justice, passionate about who has the power — but don't really love anybody in particular. Stalin and Lenin would be outstanding examples in this century.

NINE: The Path of Nonviolence

The path of nonviolence belongs to the NINE. This is true on two levels, basically because they don't engage as quickly as the rest of us do.

First, they allow time and freedom for connectedness. The rest of us don't find ourselves taking a defensive posture around NINEs. That's why everybody likes NINEs. You never need to defend yourself around them. They allow. Because they allow to be whatever is, they allow the possibility of nonviolent connecting responses. NINEs don't create enemies or force us into a defensive position.

Second, they're natural nonviolent resisters. For them, passive-aggressiveness is an art form. You don't have to teach nonviolent resistance to NINEs; that's normally the way they operate in this world. When they think some event or situation is stupid or dumb, they just don't show up. They won't write you a nasty letter; they just don't come.

I saw this in religious life for years. If the NINEs knew that a boring presider was scheduled to celebrate the community mass and his homily was certain to be terrible, they wouldn't complain. They just didn't appear at mass that day. They found something better to do. That was their quiet form of resistance to a stupid world.

"Sometimes the world is really foolish and useless," explains a NINE. "When it gets too bad, I just check out. I look for the next thing to do."

NINEs are usually ready for the next thing. That's the nonviolent gift of the NINE. You see it in Archbishop Hunthausen: I talk about him as the patron saint of NINEs. When he saw that the foreign policy of this country was stupid and we were using our weapons to kill people, he just said, "I'm not paying my war taxes anymore." Even the pope wasn't going to change his mind. That's nonviolent resistance.

NINEs can be veritable donkeys. I should have used the donkey as the symbol for the nine. When NINEs dig their heels in, when they choose their decisive action, they can be stubborn as mules. They sometimes display a sort of "cynical trust" in the world. They seem to say, "It's not worth changing, but that's okay. I'm going to enjoy it as it is, relax in it." Nobody else can put cynicism and trust together except NINEs.

But they have to make a decision about what they want to do in the world and bring themselves to focus on it. When they do, NINEs become clear-minded persons. It usually takes most of their life to finally reach that focus, because for the most part they procrastinate and put it off. But when they focus, they are well on their way.

Theirs is a quiet path, but it is also a path that connects to other paths and has the capacity to bring many of us along with them. In this sense, they are really power leaders. They don't threaten any of us. "I think I can walk with him," we say. "I think I can trust him. He's not going to pull any surprises out of the bag."

Decisions for the NINEs will come slowly, but when they do come, they will be clear and simple with no need for second guessing.

•

I hope this description of the nine paths of the Enneagram helps you to trust yourself and one another in a new way. Above all, I hope it enables you to see your gift.

Remember, as Pascal said, "You have no choice; you must place your bet."

Part II

Enneagram Panels: Handling Stress and Betrayal

6

EIGHTs

In the following chapters, we hear from panels of participants who have the same Enneagram number. The panels offer their reflections in turn, grouped around the three centers: Gut, Heart, and Head, beginning with the Gut numbers: EIGHT, NINE, and ONE. Each Enneagram panel shares what they discovered about themselves in responding to two questions. The instructions I gave to the panels are as follows:

•

The first question is:

How do you react in situations of real stress or sudden crisis?

We know that in times of stress and crisis most of us slip into our worst self, our compulsive self, the self we are used to. Now, of course, in this group, I presume everyone is redeemed already, so you no longer live in your old self. [*Laughter*] What I ask you to do is to sacrifice that "redemption" a bit and, for the sake of pedagogy and education, to illustrate for us some of the compulsive energy that your number slips into in situations of stress and sudden crisis.

The second question is:

How do you deal with betrayal in your life?

Imagine a scenario in which you have been personally betrayed by a friend. The betrayal could be legal, financial, sexual — whatever you can relate to emotionally.

In the spiritual life, betrayal is a bridge every human must cross. It isn't something that just "might" happen. Spiritually, betrayal seems necessary for the breaking of false innocence.

Jesus was betrayed three times: by Judas, by Peter, and on the cross. Though most people may not reflect on the fact, Jesus on the cross feels betrayed by God his Father. It is only when Jesus deals with his betrayals that he finally breaks into a love of the real, an embrace of reality as it is.

How we deal with betrayals is a crucial issue that I want to address. Betrayals either make you bitter or they make you profound. During life, we will all be betrayed by someone we thought would never betray us. The spiritually profound question is not whether we've been betrayed — there is no question that betrayals will happen — but how we react and respond at the moment of betrayal and during the time afterward. That is why I chose it as a question for all of us to use.

Your responses to these questions will give us a very deep understanding of the nine Enneagram numbers. I ask you not to offer us idealized, sanitized, or redeemed Enneagram answers. I ask you to speak from your gut, heart, and head.

First EIGHT

I wrote my responses to make sure I wasn't tempted to put a better face on my answers than are written here.

In a real crisis, I do several things. One is to mentally withdraw from anybody helping me; I abandon my resources because I'm sure I don't need them anyway.

Next, I begin to feel like I'm passionate and on fire emotionally: sort of a "sick omnipotence" is a good way to describe it.

Third, in times of crisis I'm prone to addictive behavior. This is something I've been able to name in just the last few years; I've noticed how feeding my addiction serves as a way to cool down the fire.

Another way I describe myself as an EIGHT in times of stressful difficulty is that I take a "junkyard dog" approach to life. I welcome a worthy foe whom I duel with or try to intimidate. As a junkyard dog I pump lots and lots of adrenaline, so much that I recognize no other authority except myself. I don't need anyone else to tell me what to do because I know what to do. My power is sufficient.

Also, I avoid and pull away from people who might be able to look through my façade and see my softness and my gentle core.

Regarding betrayal by a personal friend, my immediate reaction is: "How dare he or she! How dare anyone do that to me!" They have made a terrible mistake in thinking that I am someone they can mess with.

In dealing with betrayal long-term, I have lots of other reactions. I have a sense that I could eat this person up, destroy them, wipe them out. Whether or not I ever literally do this, they are "done" as far as I am concerned. They are through forever. I picture the image of pulling up the moat on them, letting the alligators out, and saying to them, "It's over."

When I'm in this state, I stay blind to any of their good qualities, so I can remain convinced that they deserved to be eliminated from my life.

At the same time, I sort of decide that I won't ever again let myself be so vulnerable that I get hurt.

Second EIGHT

My name is Chris. I'm an EIGHT.

In situations of stress or crisis, I feel very calm but energized, and I don't show any emotion outwardly. If I do feel fear, I hide it. I hate feeling fearful.

As energized, I feel very responsible and quickly get to *the* plan. I am quite sure that my plan is *the* plan; it never crosses my mind that there could be any other plan. I start to give orders and take charge. I never doubt for a minute that I can handle whatever it is.

Only much, much later will I have some emotional reaction to the stress. I may even fall apart from it.

But I don't connect these two opposite reactions. The second reaction is so delayed that I don't recognize the "taking charge" as having anything to do with the "falling apart."

On the question of betrayal, my first reaction is to zoom in with a verbal attack on this betrayer. I feel quite sure I can convince them of the error of their ways, that I want to bring justice to this situation, and I want to make it right. "And," my husband adds, "I can cut you off at the knees."

In the long term, I simply feel great discomfort when things are not right. The memory of the event won't go away from me. I continue to grieve over it because I don't know how to make it right. It feels unjust and I feel powerless. And I hate that feeling of powerlessness.

At times like that, it seems as though all of my emotions are showing and that everyone can tell how I'm feeling. It's as though my emotions are all hanging right out there for all to see.

I long to have the situation made right. I visualize my betrayer coming to me and saying, "Oh, I was wrong," and me fixing it. But when this doesn't happen, I'm pretty much consumed by my rage. To me it is outrageous that this betrayal is so unfair and unjust and wasn't made right.

On that, I hit bottom and really feel ashamed.

Third EIGHT

When real stress or crisis happens, I feel nothing emotionally. I have no feelings at all. But physically, I experience a tremendous rush. My voice trembles and I get a tremendous adrenal surge. Behaviorally, I do my duty.

I can think of two crises that may be interesting to reflect on.

During the Vietnam era, I took care of casualties as a surgeon and I never felt any emotion. I stuffed my feelings inside and dealt with them through alcohol. This was very effective in enabling me not to deal with the stress. I've been a recovering alcoholic for the last fifteen years.

The second crisis was an airplane crash in Sioux City that I had to deal with. Again, I had the same deadened emotions, the same physical rush, and I did my duty. But afterwards, I became very, very vulnerable because I felt it all emotionally. I was paying the price of not feeling for the last forty years.

That was a real change for me. I became much more vulnerable than I used to be — and I don't always like that. I missed my alcohol — my anesthesia — but I really didn't desire to drink because I knew how disastrous that would be.

Betrayal? Betray me?

With my rage, I wouldn't advise it.

I have an immediate rage that terrifies me so much that I shut down instantly. I don't know what my rage is really capable of and I hope I never find out.

Following the rage comes resentment. My standard comment to myself is, "Don't get mad, get even."

For an alcoholic, resentment is the sure path to self-destruction. An alcoholic will start drinking from resentment sooner than from anything else. Resentment is absolute poison. The cure for resentment is a standard one, as your sponsor will tell you, "You have to pray for the person you hate."

I do it. I pray, but I don't mean it. [*Great laughter*] Still I do it. Amazingly, you don't have to mean it; you can fake your prayer and it still works.

Fourth EIGHT

My name is John. Naturally, an EIGHT would stand up to address a group, because that way you'll notice me and I'll feel more powerful.

Just doing this presentation in front of you is stressful. Acting redeemed in public is very stressful. But, blessedly, I didn't think about what I would say. You should never give an EIGHT time to think about anything.

So, I'm under stress now. What is my reaction?

My first reaction is: "Are you friendly? Or are you my enemy?" I will engage you immediately, the way I do best, with words. I know some words will come out of me that will be provocative. You have to get ready because I'm going to try to touch you at a gut level, out of something that I'm struggling for.

I'm frustrated right now talking to you, but when I get the word that I've touched your gut, I'm going to become peaceful.

My energy is going to move at you, even though I'm afraid. Everyone talks about EIGHTs being fearless. It's not so; I'm a fearful EIGHT. Nevertheless, even when I'm afraid, the First Marine Division inside me is going to move toward you. And I'm going to touch you at a very primitive level. I always do.

When people are around me, they get nervous — and they ought to [*Laughter*] because that's EIGHT energy they're around.

When this EIGHT is angry, at least I feel strong. And it comes out of me. When I try to subdue it, it comes out of me anyway. And I'm going to reach for a word that is going to touch a word in you that's going to hit you at an unconscious level, and you're going to feel uneasy. When that happens, we're engaged, and I'm comfortable. That's EIGHTness.

I'm a lot like a large friendly dog that comes into your living room. If you don't pet me, I might bite you. That's an EIGHT's energy.

I lean toward SEVEN most of the time, which tells me, "When people are socially irresponsible, be nice and make them like you."

Regarding betrayal, I agree: Don't try it on me.

Resentment? I can identify with that. But we EIGHTs don't receive resentment; we give it — all the time.

My first reaction to betrayal is decidedly unspiritual: it's to get back. And there's something that pops up inside me spontaneously, like those guys in the French Revolution who everyday gave the executioner a list that said, "These fellows must be executed today for the good of the State." The executioner instinct is in me first, before I think of God. That's the impossible part of an EIGHT that needs to be redeemed.

I'm an EIGHT who happens to extrovert my mess. My best friends are ONEs because they are charged up with this internal fear. I externalize their fear, and that gets me in trouble.

My messes are documented: "You can see what he does," they say. "He's heavy."

I turn to God and say, "I'd like to be above this."

God replies, "You're above nothing. This is you."

Richard, your opening prayer gave me peace, because that is the place I'd like to come to. When I can come to accept who I am and not try to change that, that's what God loves and what God is working with. I'm God's bag of tricks. This is me. Here I am with all of my stuff. When I come to peace, I see it all as gift. And for that I'm grateful.

Discussion

Richard: Thank you, all. You were so-o-o-o conscientious, you all kept to your two minutes. I didn't think anybody would do that.

We have a few more minutes to share with the EIGHTs, if people would like to ask them any questions.

Perhaps I can start off with a question for Chris. Near the end of your time, you said you felt ashamed. That isn't typical of an EIGHT. Usually EIGHTs don't feel shame. Would you explain a bit what you meant by that?

EIGHT (Chris): I can get to a state with my rage and my anger that it just embarrasses me. I feel shame that I have lost control. That's probably where the shame comes from: that I haven't been more disciplined, that I haven't controlled things more, that I've let the situation get out of hand.

Richard: Can the rest of you EIGHTs relate to that response?

EIGHT (Pat): That's right on. I feel a shame too, but I think I'm more ashamed when my plan doesn't work. [*Laughter*] I'm ashamed because I understand power and I haven't used it well.

Richard: Shame is normally more like a ONE response. The reason you EIGHTs are so powerful is that you usually don't pull back into shame; you usually just stay out there with it. You do get upset — but not ashamed — that it didn't work.

EIGHT (Chris): That's true. I'm upset that I didn't do it right, that I didn't make it happen.

Richard: You didn't make your power happen.

EIGHT (Pat): The reason is EIGHTs have a sense of being master or mistress of the power politic, and when we don't do well what we know we can do well, we feel ineffective.

Richard: I did hear in most of you a certain fear of your rage. The rage seems so strong that you're almost afraid of what it could do if you let it.

EIGHT (Chris): Absolutely.

EIGHT (Pat): Yes. That's why I never allowed myself to hit my children.

Richard: Anybody else? Any questions from the floor?

Floor: I would like to ask the EIGHTs, What really gets under your skin?

EIGHT: Absolutely, positively, without question — anyone who's abusive. Anybody who abuses someone who is smaller than they are, particularly a child or a small animal. Whenever it happens, it takes me into rage.

EIGHT: My volunteer work is in the field of child abuse. Children are whom I really want to protect.

EIGHT: For years, before I came to the Center, my work was in child abuse.

EIGHT: This may be very surprising to some people, but that response is very common among EIGHTs. If I'm in a public place and some parent is hectoring his or her child, it's almost impossible for me to control myself. It's an excruciating experience to stand there and watch it happen. I identified this response most recently in viewing the Romero film the other day. During that powerful scene where the peasant farmer comes in from the countryside and sees his son lying dead, I was just filled with a rage and a fear and a desire to strike out.

Richard: Maybe one more question?

Floor: I have a comment on the EIGHTs' responses. I think the shame was felt more by the women. In EIGHTs there seems to be a strong masculine energy, but it's not okay for women to display this masculine energy in our culture. So women might feel certain cultural pressures that the men would not experience. Which leads to my question: When do you experience your vulnerability? And how are you most comfortable expressing it, even though it's generally uncomfortable?

EIGHT (Male): I'm usually afraid to talk when I feel vulnerable, for fear I might cry.

EIGHT (Female): For me, crying used to be the hardest thing. When I tell the story of what happened to me in my year of therapy, I say that what I learned was how to cry and how to cry in public — and to let it be.

EIGHT (Female): How to cry with people I trust and am close to. But I know I show a tremendous amount of vulnerability with my grandchildren — with little people. They don't have to be my grandchildren, as long as they're babies or little things.

Floor: How do we approach EIGHTs when you are in your rage? Give us advice.

EIGHT: I wouldn't want this statement used against me, but I'm absolutely disarmed when someone just says to me, "You know, that really, really hurt me." Then my rage kind of crumbles, because inside I really am a soft person who doesn't want to hurt people. In fact, I'm often surprised that anyone feels intimidated or hurt by me. I'm just not aware of that.

EIGHT: My greatest need is just to be heard. All I want is for someone to tell me they really heard what I was saying and understood what I was doing.

EIGHT: Don't try to take my rage from me. My mother used to say, "Step on your lip." I resent those words to this day.

EIGHT: I had a recent experience with someone disarming me.

There's a woman, my age, I talk to about once a week; she's very direct and not frightened of me. She just names my state of mind. "What's this?" she asks, and then she names it. Her response is usually very frank but it is also very calming. What I realize is that she respects the EIGHTness in me. Respect is what she gives me.

Richard: EIGHTs respect you when they see you're not intimidated by them. If you'll just stand face-to-face with them, neither trying to overpower them nor taking the lower ground but just coming on to them as a peer, if you do that, they'll respect you.

Thank you very much. Now let's move on to the NINE panel.

7

NINEs

I thought we'd let the NINEs get their turn over right away, so they can relax the rest of the day. We'll ask them the same two questions we asked the EIGHTs:

First, how do you deal with crisis or a stress situation?

Second, how do you deal with betrayal?

First NINE

The way I react in a situation of real stress or sudden crisis is not to notice there is a crisis going on. It's very important to me to appear calm, because ever since I was a small child I took some pride in appearing calm. But underneath my calm exterior, I am not calm. I'm nervous, and I'm afraid my nervousness might show, so I do a lot of withdrawing.

One of my ways of withdrawing is not to notice there is a crisis.

I can be quite addicted. Many years ago I was addicted to alcohol and cigarettes. Even though I don't drink or smoke now, when I'm in a crisis, I might start paging through magazines or newspapers.

Once the crisis is visible to me and clear in my head, I'm very likely to start obsessing, particularly at night, when I'll simply keep spinning in my head what's going on, over and over and over again. During this time, I'm trying to figure out what to do about the crisis or how to manage it. For example, I'm thinking, "What letter can I write that will simply turn the key and cause the whole matter to be solved?"

While one side of my response to crisis is withdrawal, the other side is quite active decisiveness. When I'm really engaged in a crisis and know what I want to do, I'll confront it, I'll write letters, and I'll try to get to the other side of it.

In terms of betrayal, I would describe myself as crazily understanding. When I'm betrayed, I can be very calm and try to understand what has happened and why and what my own part in it has been and how I contributed.

There is still another part to my response. Once I'm past the understanding of the betrayal, I can have delayed reactions. For example, one delayed reaction is that years later I realize I have a kind of frozen resentment that's just eating away at me. Sometimes it's not quite eating away; it's more like I become aware that the resentment is there, and it becomes something I carry with me about this person.

Another way in which I respond over time is violently. I may even get explosively angry if the resentment builds up.

Second NINE

I'm Mary, and I share a lot in common with Frank, who just spoke. But I'm an introverted NINE, so when I deal with stress, it carries a little different flavor with it.

What happens initially is the crisis pulls against my senses. For the most part, as you know, a NINE will sort of float along with life and be passive. But faced with a really severe or sudden crisis, my sensing ability comes right into focus. Emotionally, I'm right there. I may not do anything about it, but I'm really in tune with what's going on.

What I do is rehearse, retreat, and then process it. If the emotion is strong enough or I can sense clearly enough what's going on, then I will react immediately and be decisive. But it takes a really clear crisis for me to make a decision about it.

At a betrayal, my first reaction would be disbelief. It would be a shock. I would say to myself, "I'm so trusting, why would this person betray me?"

I would feel violated, but then I would withdraw and process what actually happened. After that, I would probably do some acting out, either by eating or verbally abusing whoever happens to be around.

From that, I would move into a deep sense of loss, because at that point I would feel that the relationship has broken down somehow, either because of me or the other person.

I would really grieve over losing whatever was there, because being dishonest with me or violating my trust is pretty sacred for me. To build that trust back up again would take a lot of energy.

Over a longer period of time, I would sense there is some kind of a flaw in the person who betrayed me, something in them that caused them to break that confidence or violate that trust. There would still be a sense of loss — a really deep sense.

But I wouldn't know how to rebuild that relationship at all. I would not even know how to entertain that thought.

If I met that person again, chances are I would just act very cool and collected. I would not be very interactive with them. I might tolerate them, but I would not confront.

Third NINE

First of all, I want to apologize for being here, because I don't want to be here. It was not by choice that I am here. There were only three of us NINEs in the entire group.

Did I just then behave like a NINE?

I'm an extroverted NINE and I'm a verbal thinker. What goes through my head comes right out my mouth like a bullet. If I think it, it gets said.

Emotionally, when I get into a situation of crisis or stress, I rage, I scream, and I'm probably verbally abusive. I threaten. I come apart.

But, rather than confront the person and find a healthy way to deal with my emotional anger, I retreat. Or I become ill. Or I'll go to bed for a week and stew about it. [Laughter]

Lately after a crisis, I do a lot of inner work.

I had the most marvelous experience here a few weeks ago. Through the guidance of a priest, I was able to take myself through the rage and destruction to the healing, and finally through the resolving. It took me about six hours.

As for personal betrayals, I don't have them. From my position as a NINE, I don't get that involved, so I don't get betrayed. I have a lot of friends, but I don't have personal friends — someone I'm really enmeshed with. This way, if they leave me, they've lost a friend. I'm indifferent about the loss. I'll pick up another friend. [Laughter]

Usually, I just cut them off. I don't need the relationship.

When I took my first Enneagram workshop, Richard compared the NINE with an elephant and a caterpillar. I'm that little caterpillar. In the years I've been able to see myself, I'm always on the fence just moving along — a little fuzzy.

I could also be a butterfly, flying over here to do this and flying over there to do that. If someone ruffles my wings, I'll go back into my cocoon where it's safe.

But if someone steps on that caterpillar, I become like an elephant. It takes a long time to get me into my elephant, but once I become elephant, I'll tromp through. I can keep tromping forever. One time, I drove through five states before I came to. [Laughter] Yes, I finally ended up down here in Albuquerque. [Laughter] That was my original destination, but I drove thorough Kansas first and then Oklahoma to get here.

In Albuquerque I made a retreat, cooled off, then went home. When I got home, my husband said, "Great! She's well again."

So, I live out the true life of the elephant and caterpillar.

I have a great deal of trouble getting involved in women's guilds at church, because those women drive me crazy. I'm willing to take part in the groups and get fed off them, but when it comes my turn to be president or leader, I don't have the time. I don't want to be involved.

That's who I am!

Discussion

Richard: Frank made an important observation — the obsessive thinking that seems to be a common pattern for all Gut people. It's the Gut person's way of working in the Head. We Guts can obsess all night long. That obsessing is not unusual for us.

Any questions?

Floor: I deal a lot with a NINE. Because this person is so affable and easy to get along with, when I come on angrily, I immediately feel guilty. As NINEs, how do you want someone like me to approach you if there is a conflict?

NINE: I would want you to be very honest and direct.

NINE: I would, too.

NINE: I don't want any games. I want the truth right on.

Richard: That's their EIGHT wing responding. Both wings of the NINE are very powerful for them. They would appreciate directness. I'm sure they're right.

Floor: What if that NINE doesn't see a conflict? Suppose we're in a conflict situation, and the NINE says, "Oh, it's going to be all right. Everything is really okay"?

Richard: The pain many of us experience in dealing with NINEs is when they are unable to see the problem or the conflict.

NINE: I can be helpful if I know what the conflict is that you're having. If you can be very clear about your problem and how I'm connected with it, then I can recognize the problem.

Richard: It sounds as though you [the questioner] are dealing with an unhealthy NINE who's into a cocoon and telling you, "I'm not coming out." The NINEs here can't really speak to your question, because they've come out of their cocoons.

NINE: Another way for you to help a NINE see the conflict would be to offer a number of options or different ways of resolving the conflict. That way, as a NINE, I could choose an option to which I could relate and which made sense to me.

Floor: Do NINEs project their emotions — like anger — onto another person? Or would they tend to own their own anger?

Richard: That's a most difficult position for a NINE.

NINE: I think I'm rather specialized in emotions. In certain areas, I can get to be a lot like a very suspicious SIX. For example, if I am facing difficulty in a sexual relationship, I can get into a strong SIX position. I usually don't, but I could.

Floor: When you're in your passive-aggressive mode, what is the best way for others to get through that cloud? What's our best first move?

NINE: For me, just leave me alone to work it out, to go through the process. If you come at me and nag, it won't work.

Richard: She'll become a donkey. I'm sure she's giving you an honest and helpful response. When NINEs are in their passive-aggressive posture, don't try to pull them out too quickly. They've got to stay in it for a while.

NINE: I want my husband to love me and caress me and hear me and understand me. I don't want him to let me go off.

Richard: Do you relate only to your husband that way, or is that a more general observation?

NINE: It's more general. I'm always looking for that healer.

Richard: Even when you're just sitting there with your hurt?

NINE: Yes.

Floor: I have an EIGHT daughter married to a NINE. One of their major difficulties follows this pattern: She looks like she's harping at him, but when I watch for his response, he'll go and do something, like pick up a magazine, look at it, and get lost in it. He never gets to where he's going. Is his behavior something you can relate to?

NINE: For me, if the harping — or whatever — is not important and doesn't grab my attention, I will just tune out. I will look like I'm right here, but I'm really out there somewhere. I may look present and may even be perceived as a good listener, but if the situation is not grabbing my attention or I don't think it's worthwhile and don't want to put energy into it, I'm not with you at all.

NINE: A NINE simply doesn't want to get involved. The way I see it, others don't want to get involved with my problems and I don't want to get involved with their problems. I've got all I can do to handle my own. [*Laughter*]

Floor: What's the most loving thing a person can do for a NINE?

NINE: What means most to me is any kind of gesture that represents acceptance. That's what's powerful for me.

NINE: Just allow me to be me — whether I'm passive-aggressive, whether I withdraw. I feel loved when you can do whatever it takes to be able to just sit with whatever I'm doing.

NINE: Unconditional love.

Richard: All God's people long for unconditional love most of all. And we need to experience it down here, in the gut.

Floor: Do NINEs tend to choose friends who are mostly active people with problems? Or are they calm, soothing people like you seem to be? If you have friends who are outgoing and you are not outgoing, do you have conflicts with them? If they express a need or feel an emotion, do you just tune out? What do you do? What happens? Do you get involved?

NINE: That's a fairly easy question for me to answer, since many of my friends are outgoing or very extroverted. One of my best friends is an extroverted EIGHT. I welcome that energy. I like to be invited. I like to be pulled out of what I am, although I like the option of saying no. I like their energy; I like to get pulled along with it. So there really isn't a conflict.

Richard: That's also my observation of NINEs. Because they are not self-starters, they're eager for someone from the outside to give them the juice, and they will usually go along with the juice, which is why the rest of us like NINEs. They will accept our energy and flow with it. They normally like to have some juicy friends.

NINE: I find that I select women friends that are a lot like me, people who keep their distance. They don't get involved with me, and we keep our space between us — all the time.

NINE: Let me balance that observation. I like to be with people I can get involved with. I also get into relationships with people who have troubles and conflicts, because I like participating in situations where I feel I can be helpful.

Floor: I think I have a strong NINE wing, so I'd like to hear some personal accounts of what engages you. What does it take for you to get going?

NINE: Injustice, definitely, on any level, because a NINE is always trying to balance things. Situations that are way out of balance will spark me off immediately. It could be a personal problem among other people that will engage me; I'll try to help them understand their problem and reach a peaceful solution or reconciliation.

NINE: For me — and this probably contradicts what other NINEs might say because I'm an extrovert — I need someone to engage me, otherwise I'll sit back. Once I'm motivated from outside or someone else puts that challenge in front of me, then I can take the ball and really go with it. Once I'm finished with that game or whatever project we're doing, I'll sit back and relax or go on a trip. I'll wait until something comes along again. I always need to have that outside force to get me going.

Floor: My oldest daughter is a NINE and a teacher. She acts much as you describe. When there's a confrontation with other teachers at school, she says, "My emotions are too strong. I cannot say anything at the time. I withdraw." Then, two days later she will call me because she has thought through the confrontation. Then she goes on and on.

Richard: At times like those, NINEs can give you infinite detail. They can be just like FIVEs in that regard.

Floor (continues): Right. I don't know any of those teachers at school she's talking about, but as a SIX and her mother, I always wonder what I should do. When it goes on too long, I sometimes try to change the subject, but she won't. She just stays on it. How can I help her?

Richard: If I may speak? At the point when NINEs are going into all kinds of detail, they have lost their focus. They're displaying their loss of focus verbally. What NINEs have to work for is focus. When they lose it, they can bore you in conversation with all their unnecessary detail. And you say, "I don't want to hear all this. Why would you think I would want to hear all this?"

NINE: It seems to me when I'm in that state, I need someone to ask me, "What do you want to do about it?" I may not have an immediate answer for you, but I need that shove to get to the place where I realize what I want to do about it.

Floor: You may have answered my question already. I was in a support group with a NINE who frustrated the hell out of me. Working together in a support group, you expect everybody to contribute, but he saw no talents within himself, nothing seemed to excite him, he didn't know what he was going to do or what he was good at. He was out of touch with past or future, just sort of floating. I like closure; he had no closure — and no openings. Subsequently, our support group took an Enneagram workshop, and he discovered he was a NINE. This led me to a better understanding of him, but he was obviously a very unredeemed NINE. My question is: what is the route out for a NINE?

NINE: For years before I knew anything about the Enneagram, one of my favorite book titles was Kierkegaard's *Purity of Heart Is to Will One Thing*. When I realized I was a NINE, what was most important to me was the idea of decisive action as the way of redemption for a NINE. I think that's what Kierkegaard's title is all about. I think NINEs need somehow or other to discover what they can act on in a way that is really meaningful to them. How to get them there is another question, but I think that's what's necessary to get them out.

NINE: That's always the inner struggle of the NINE: Who am I? When I first went for counseling, I said to the counselor, "You know, I'm fifty years old and I don't know who the hell I am." I had brought up four kids, I'd done everything right according to the church, and I still didn't know who I was.... I think identity is a real struggle with NINEs, and that's why we flit like butterflies. We need someone to come along and kind of guide us into redemption. That guide will be our redemption.

Richard: You finally have to do it by yourself, but you often need an outsider to get you started. The way you're saying it, you sound more like a SIX. But I think I know the way you mean it., which is that you need some help from outside yourself to get your juices going.

NINE: Tell me, then, am I a NINE?

Richard: Is someone telling you that?

NINE: I'm asking you. Am I a NINE?

Richard: Yes, I think you're a NINE. You probably just happened to get a lot of good church training. [*Laughter*] I think Frank put it well in quoting that great line from Kierkegaard's book, *Purity of Heart Is to Will One Thing*. I'm saying a similar thing about all the paths, and it's especially true for NINEs. All their life is an avoidance of focus and almost a fear that there is no focus to be had. They fear it because they have a hard time finding focus within themselves.

A more dramatic way of saying this is that NINEs doubt they have a soul. They doubt their own importance, which is part of what we perceive as their humility. They never demand their own way because they're not sure there is a way.

They become jacks of all trades and masters of none, the universal joint that goes with the flow. This makes it very easy for the rest of us to be with NINEs, but sometimes they're a real sadness to themselves because they're not sure they matter in the world.

On the positive side, you could just as easily say they, in fact, have an honest image of themselves, since we're all little creatures on this earth. No one knows our littleness better than a NINE.

While some of the rest of us have to be forcibly convinced that we are little and unimportant, you don't have to ego-strip a NINE. You really don't. Their problem is more on the other side: they just don't think they're that big a deal.

Thank you, NINEs, for being a big deal to us.

8

ONEs

Now, let's hear from my kind of people, the ONEs. These I'll certainly understand. Talk to us, first, about handling stress and crisis. Then tell us how you deal with betrayal.

First ONE

I'm Pat, and I'm going first because I have to be a good little girl.

I'm terrified. None of the ONEs in our group last night would volunteer to be on the panel.

When I was in high school, I was nominated to be on the student council, and I conned the school into letting me give my acceptance speech over the public address system so I didn't have to appear in front of the student body. And here I am in front of you.

How do I react in times of stress and crisis? I become emotionally agitated, impatient, really irritated, but not outright angry. And I try to hide it all, but it comes out in little ways. For example, I might express it by saying, "Someone didn't do what they were supposed to have done."

I then try to figure out who that someone was.

I go on from there, take over the situation, and solve the problem., because I know how to do it right.

If there's a crisis going on, I tend to be able to jump in, take control, organize things, change the game plan, and do whatever has to be done at the time to make the thing work. That's what I tend to do in a crisis.

On the other question — betrayal — I'd just like to give an example. During high school I had a close personal friend. Twenty years later, I found out he had sexually abused two of my children — two boys. It was very devastating for me. I was hurt; I felt betrayed. I don't think I came to anger until much later.

Instead, I went into my ONE role immediately, because I knew that something had to be done and the right thing had to be done, not only for him but for my children. We went through the court process, and about a year later the gentleman ended up in the state penitentiary.

75

On the other hand, because I have a strong TWO wing, the prosecution of him was very difficult for me. During the court proceedings, I learned a lot about who he was and what was wrong. He was a pedophile, a very sick man. I felt compassion for him. My TWO energy was there — I had known him for years and he had been a good friend — and would not let me be angry. It was an interesting experience to go through.

As far as how I reacted to it long-term, I gradually lost the anger. But, interestingly, the last two times the man has been up for parole, I've had mixed emotions about it, but both times I have chosen to keep him in prison because I thought of society — someone else's child, my own children's children — and felt this person just had to stay in prison.

Yet my TWO side wants to let him out. It's a real conflict for me. It was very difficult for me to go to those parole hearings. It was very difficult every time I had to go back to the court and stand there and know I was keeping behind bars a person who had grown up in a very wealthy county, in a loving home, who was very sick but not by his own fault.

Second ONE

My name is Dan. In times of stress — like now — I think what happens is a chain reaction.

First, I immediately stuff my emotions; I never let them become public.

Then I go back and forth between my behavior and my emotions, what I feel and what I do. Again, immediately, I stuff my emotions.

Then I look to see if it's a problem that's within my scope to solve. If it's not, then I don't do anything. I don't want to try if I can't do it right. But I tend to think I can do it right.

When I think I'm the one who can solve the problem, I immediately become the do-er, the organizer, the care-giver, the take-charge person. And I get focused into that.

If it's an extended crisis, I'll slowly begin to shut down so I can deal with the emotional part of it that I had stuffed, otherwise those emotions will come out later in sick ways.

On betrayal, I thought I'd tell a short story, too.

When I was younger, I had a trusted friend named Roy. When I trust, I trust completely. The two of us had a mutual friend, Joe. One day, Joe came over to Roy's house, but I didn't know he was there. Joe said he would go into the closet (so I wouldn't know he was there), and he wanted Roy to ask me what I thought of Joe. Roy asked me about Joe and I told him what I honestly felt. All of a sudden Joe burst out of the closet.

I felt betrayed by my friend Roy. I looked at him and wondered how this could have possibly happened since I had trusted him.

True to ONE form, I stuffed my emotions.

When I do that, I in fact probably don't even realize how deeply I am hurt.

The steps are sort of like this: I feel undercut, I don't react, I try to be a good person and say, "Oh, that's okay," but deep inside it's painful.

The long-term reaction is, not only will I never trust this person again, but I won't trust people in general ever again. I don't want to risk betrayal ever again.

Maybe it's just a personal thing with me, but I always have a problem with trust, because when I trust I trust completely. But if my trust is ever betrayed, I cut it off and never trust again.

Third ONE

I think standing up here is hard for all of us because we want to be perfect. We want you to think we're perfect people giving all the right answers. More so for me, because I feel a strong TWO wing, so I think: "Am I a ONE or am I a TWO? I don't want to give the wrong impression here."

First of all, how do I react under stress?

I think I shut down.

If I have an opportunity to go off and work it out, I'll do that. I try to do things like cook, swim, clean — I love to clean.

But if I'm in a stressful situation and have to stay in it, I am almost in another world. It hits me in my stomach and I almost black out. I'm trying to keep the other person thinking I'm still there. I try to be the best little girl I can.

If I can't work it out, sometimes I'll say nasty things on my way out the door. I want to avoid the situation.

In the past when I've stuffed my emotions, I have been known to throw things, believe it or not. This is the anger coming out that I can't afford to identify, because good little girls aren't allowed to be angry.

While listening to everyone discussing how they handle crisis, I began to think that reactions have a lot to do with whether you're an introvert or an extrovert, whether you're a woman or a man.

With betrayal, again, I act like I almost can't believe it happened.

I haven't been able to trust people because I think, "Well, these poor people. They're human, not perfect like me, so of course they're not going to be able to be trustworthy." I just take it as a matter of life.

I can trust and I'm very trustworthy — which I may not be, but I feel I am.

When betrayal happens a second time, I shut down. I need time to figure it out. "Who's wrong? Maybe I was wrong? Maybe I didn't do the right thing? Or maybe they didn't?"

Again, because of my TWO wing, I am very relational. In growing up, I learned that if you're a good Christian person you're going to have good relationships. And when a relationship doesn't work out, I tend to blame myself and try to figure out reasons why it didn't work.

I do have trouble relating to that person again. They don't know this, because I'm sweet and wonderful and nice, but I'll never trust them again, even though they try hard to make up.

I don't like that about myself, but that's the way it is. And that's not perfect.

Fourth ONE

What I usually do in a sudden crisis is experience an emotional release, and I cry. The tears are so gushing that I often think that my kidney lies behind my eyes. On first impulse I usually get very frustrated, and then I start to pray, "Oh, please give me some help here!"

And then I get a really big adrenaline push.

Behaviorally, I'll usually start cleaning. [*Much laughter*] I try to whistle while I work and, if that doesn't succeed, I'll go outside and start pulling weeds or doing gardening, which is something I really enjoy. If I can swing something like a golf club, that usually helps, too.

When I'm betrayed by a personal friend, I'll feel terribly hurt. After all, I've chosen this friend, so I can't understand why they would do such a thing to me. I can forgive them, but it's hard to forget. However, I forget that it is hard to forget, and the memory of the betrayal keeps coming back. When it does, I'll say to myself, "I don't know why they did this to me."

I will try to look at both sides of the betrayal.

As a child, I loved sitting on teeter-totters. If I didn't have a friend on the other side, I'd just sit in the middle and try to balance myself. I would hope that someone my size would happen by and sit on the other side. Then we'd have a lot more fun, 'cause having fun is what I want to do.

Discussion

Richard: As a ONE, I really liked that teeter-totter image. ONEs have a mania for balance. I've never heard anyone give a metaphor for it as apt as that. We saw the need for balance quite strongly in you ONEs. It's expressed in the fact that you want to see and understand the other side, the other person's view.

We ONEs are reasonable to a fault. I noticed this quality in all four of you ONEs. We cut the flow of emotions in order to be reasonable, so serious and conscientious are we.

How often ONEs use expressions like "right" and "That wasn't the way to do it." We're always balancing and correcting things. The devil's advocate energy never stops working in ONEs, which is why we're considered "heavies."

Notice that the rest of the group were not laughing very much at you ONEs. [*Laughter*]

ONEs give you the feeling that we're conscientious people, looking at both sides of everything and drawing the lines of judgment. Notice how the four ONEs were judging themselves. She even judged herself for judging someone else!

We ONEs are self-deadening people. You have to realize that. The hardest thing for us to learn is to let the flow go. When we do that, we can be highly creative, but it's hard to do. This is why the ONEs were afraid even to come up front and talk to the group, because they felt all of you were going to judge them the way we ONEs judge ourselves.

These four ONEs are sitting here judging themselves. Their inner conversation is full of judgments such as, "I'm not doing this right" or "I said that wrong" or "Why did I do that?" or "I'll bet I looked like a fool." Because they are so merciless on themselves, they presume you're doing the same to them. So be nice to them in your questions.

Floor: My closest friend is a ONE, and she has some dreadful things in her life to grieve: both her children have died from cystic fibrosis, and she's had two failed marriages. I love her dearly. I want so much to be able to give her permission to be angry and to grieve. I talk to her all the time, even though we live on opposite ends of this country. Can you suggest to me how I can tell this woman that it's okay to feel angry, to express her anger, and to grieve? How can I be a good friend to her?

ONE: The most growth I've had is in a friendship with a person who let me be who I really was and who let me see that a lot of the imperfections I was repressing were, as Richard said, just "cobwebs." She'd say, "Dan, come on! Look at this! It's cobwebs. Let's blow through this." And I'd say, "Yes, you're right. Why am I stuffing all this?"

I'm not saying you're not letting this person be. You can encourage them to see that whatever they're stuffing is probably something they don't like about themselves. Encourage them to let it come forward. Maybe when they really look at it, they'll see it's cobwebs, and they can just blow it away.

ONE: I was just going to say the same thing about a very dear friend I had through my whole life. I used to go to her house and just babble. I'm obsessive and I need to talk things out. It's like I have to hear what I'm thinking. I have to hear it over and over again. She was wonderful. She didn't give me a lot of direction and advice; she didn't judge, she just let me talk.

Richard: There's an absolutism about the ONE, an either/or-ness. Once someone hurts us, for example, it's really hard ever to trust that person again — and then we hate ourselves for being that way. That's how we become so self-deadened. You hate yourself for what you have done and then you hate yourself for having that attitude. It's really an impossible trap for a ONE. There's no way out of it.

We're constantly working to overcome our absolutism by being more balanced. Balance becomes our greatest gift. At their best, ONEs are extremely balanced people.

An adjective frequently applied to ONEs is "reasonable." I'll bet you would say that about all four of these ONEs. They're very reasonable people. They'd be willing to hear your side of the story because they have learned how to play the devil's advocate inside themselves and they'll do it outside, too. That's why you can normally work with a ONE. Even though you may grow tired of their heaviness, you know they will see your side. They'll go to the farthest degree to see your side of an issue — as long as they don't get trapped into their righteousness trip.

Floor: Among an office staff of five people, we've got three ONEs. I've noticed a real affinity between ONEs and EIGHTs. I'm an EIGHT. From the EIGHT's end, I think we nurture the affinity because we can recognize and identify with your anger. I'm not sure if the ONEs know what we see. I wonder if they realize how easy it is to see their anger?

ONE: I believe one of my dearest friends is an EIGHT. We both can see the anger in the other. I can see when she is getting angry, and she can sense my feelings. There again is the teeter-totter effect, the balance. The EIGHT and the ONE complement each other in that we're not trying to hurt one another.

ONE: I have a great respect for healthy EIGHTs. During the past few years, I've met a lot of them, especially women. Previously, I had met mostly unhealthy EIGHTs, and I found myself avoiding them. Finding healthy EIGHTs has helped me as a ONE, because I think EIGHTs and ONEs have a healthy respect for one another. Relating to EIGHTs has even helped me in dealing with my own anger.

Richard: You healthy EIGHTs give us permission to trust our anger, which we're so afraid to trust. In our reasonableness, we do think that you others sometimes overstate our anger. We want to say, "You could be so much more effective if you'd be a nice girl toward me" [*Laughter*] because we've tried so hard to be nice boys and girls to you.

Floor: I'm a SEVEN who's been married to a ONE husband for many years. One of the things he says I help him do is play. Also, I'm a planner. So I often combine the two qualities. I plan a ski trip or a wind-surfing trip or buy him roller blades and say, "Let's go out and be kids!" That's something that lightens him up. I was wondering if you ONEs identify with that? I guess my question is: Do you need help to get lightened up? And what lightens you up?

ONE: I can address that because I just recently married a SEVEN. I was attracted to him because he was a SEVEN and seemed to be able to bring out those things in me that I hold so tightly to myself. He does for me what you do for your husband. He calls me at times and challenges me, and definitely brings me out of myself.

ONE: I want to say that I tend to dislike SEVENs because I think they're wasting time. [*Laughter*] As a ONE, I like to know whether or not a SEVEN's playfulness is going to lead somewhere. If it's going to mean something, then it's worthwhile and I can let go of my restraint. I think.

ONE: Thirty-five years with a SEVEN has been great.

Floor: Even though a person doesn't know that he's a ONE, does trying to lighten him up help? Or is it necessary that he realize he is a ONE?

ONE: Before I recognized that I was a ONE, it was play that helped me identify my ONEness. I recognized play was very healthy for me. I felt just great when I was playing. I wasn't judging myself; I was just doing it. It was such a relief. I suspect sometimes play helps ONEs identify themselves. That's how I identified myself.

ONE: Being manipulated bothers me. Being told I should do something — like "You should play" — turns on my anger. I prefer that people would just ask, "How would you like to do this?" I prefer they would ask a question or invite me, instead of just telling me what to do.

ONE: That's what I want to say about the EIGHTs. I have a love/hate relationship with EIGHTs, which is why I stressed relating to healthy EIGHTs. In general, when I'm around EIGHTs, I feel they're going to make me do something I don't want to do. When I'm around them, I feel this anger sort of building up. But when it's an invitation and not something being forced on me, I feel okay about it.

Richard: To answer your question from my perspective, ONEs who don't know they're ONEs and who are into their ONEness will resent you pulling them into what might feel to them like silly, useless things. I can recall that when I was a young man, I was into heavy, serious things. When people invited me to play games, I'd say, "What a waste of time!" That's an unhealthy ONE, when everything that isn't dutiful, responsible, or building toward something meaningful is a waste of time. This is precisely why we ONEs need play so much. I think every ONE should be thrown on the floor and tickled at least once a day. [*Laughter*]

Floor: I was wondering about how you ONEs approach projects? Do you beat things too much? Do you find people saying to you, "Just let it go"?

Richard: We surely do. That's what I mean when I say that we're heavies. People are often saying to me, "Let go of it, Richard. Let it go."

Floor: I can give an example of that. I have two salespeople who work for me; they can sell the job, but it's never perfect enough. In the printing business, there are a lot of variables. From time to time, I have to say to these two people, "That's good enough."

Richard: Remember that much of our pickiness is really misplaced anger. When we're dissatisfied inside, we're looking for a container to hold our dissatisfaction. As long as we're not in touch with the stream of dissatisfaction inside us, we'll just keep looking for another thing to get picky about. To us ONEs, the problems seem endless, while others are asking us, "What's your problem?" [*Laughter*] All it is is one more thing we're upset about. That attitude in us is really damnable. It's no good.

Floor: After twenty-five years of marriage what's the most loving thing a THREE can do for a ONE with a TWO wing ? How can a THREE help a ONE?

ONE: Let me say up front that I find THREEs most intolerable when they aren't dealing with the truth and when the truth doesn't matter to them. For ONEs, truth and meaning are utterly important. So if you THREEs get to the heart of the matter, get real, and get rid of the masks, I think you'll engage a ONE, and then a love relationship can happen.

Richard: Normally, we ONEs look on THREEs as too smooth and too cool. We don't trust there's integrity or depth to them, because we've worked so hard for it. This is our arrogance showing itself. "You're doing it too easily. You're making it look too easy. We know it can't be that easy because it's agony for us." [*Laughter*] We want it to be agony for you, too.

Floor: Do you find in the unhealthy ONE state that it's easy to fall into workaholism?

ONE: I don't consider myself a workaholic, but I'm definitely a perfectionist. It's a different kind of strain. I've learned that I have to play, that I have to let go. I actually quit a job that was very demanding and took another job that I felt was demeaning. Although it's less stressful, I'm the perfectionist on the job. Everything I do is perfect. My boss said, "I wish I could say something bad about you." And I answered, "Do you know how hard I work so that you don't have anything bad to say about me?"

ONE: I think what looks to others like workaholism is really perfectionism. Personally, I will not cease until a job is done right.

Floor: When you ONEs find yourselves slipping up, when you find yourself into something illicit — as far as you're concerned — how do you find your balance in a healthy manner without just citing a rule or a principle and saying, "I'm not supposed to do this." How do you healthily look back on an error and ask, "What did I learn?" How do you do that?

Richard: We call what you described "nodding to the shadow." Every ONE must learn how to recognize what is bad or illicit; usually it's easy because we've been so perfect. But there's often one little area where we tend to break the rules. We feel terribly ashamed about it, but we do it nonetheless.

ONE: Whenever I notice a guilty feeling, all of a sudden it hits me that I've hurt someone. Then I have to go off somewhere and reflect on what's happened. That's probably because I'm more introverted than extroverted. When I go off, I say to myself, "By rights, you feel that you haven't been perfect." This time away is almost like journaling it through, talking to myself, and realizing God isn't expecting me to be perfect. It's a spiritual thing for me. I have to work out my guilty feelings before I can resolve the situation, because if I try to resolve things there and then, I come up the loser. What I have to do is get rid of the anger and frustration by "playing." When I come back, I have a better sense of what's been going on.

ONE: Once I get over the denial that something I did was wrong, I want to know the truth because then I can be perfect. I can integrate the truth and be a better person for it.

Floor: How important is order for you? You're talking about perfectionism, and my experience with ONEs is their homes are so perfect you're afraid to sit down; then you walk into their offices and they might be messy. Or vice versa. How important is outside order for you? [*Much laughter*]

ONE: Order seems very important to me. I don't know why I keep thinking *Good Housekeeping* or *Better Homes and Gardens* is going to arrive any minute and take pictures. But I always try to have a junk drawer. I'm working very hard on letting things go and trying to be a little more of a NINE, because I really admire that.

Richard: You both said something I've found to be true for ONEs. Nodding to our shadow is shown in our approach to order. Usually we'll have one place that we keep orderly. I don't keep my desk neat, but the rest of my house is immaculate. I don't know why, but the messy desk doesn't bother me. There's got to be one place where it's okay to break the rules. Isn't that strange?

ONE: My closet is where I break the rules. The outside has to be perfect. At one time, there couldn't be anything out of place if someone was coming to my house. It's a terrible feeling of disorientation when I'm out of order. On my job I'm bombarded with details and yet, because I can keep these million details all in order and things come out clearly, I feel good about it. But if the schedule is changed, I get really thrown. Living with a SEVEN has been very good for me because SEVENs don't even schedule such important things as motel reservations.

ONE: When you're touching order with a ONE, you're touching holy ground.

Floor: I'm having a hard time with the first ONE lady who spoke. I would like to ask you about what happened with your kids. I'm a ONE and I can't understand your behavior. You said that you didn't feel angry. I can't understand that. Is it possible that because you are such a perfectionist you deny your anger because you can't accept that you are angry? Or do you feel that you are truly not angry? Even Jesus, who had his passions well controlled, got very angry when he found those merchants at the temple. As a mother, I can't understand how you didn't feel angry when you discovered those temples — your children — had been violated.

ONE: I felt the anger and I knew I felt it, but I couldn't let it come out. That probably was the perfectionist side of me, but it's also been a sort of sick spirituality through the years. My TWO wing was really wanting to forgive him. In Matthew's Gospel it says you should visit the prisoners; here I was going to put someone in prison. I had a really hard time dealing with that. So I suppressed the anger.

At the time, a number of my friends said, "Come on, you really are angry." And I was. I was very hurt. I had been betrayed. I had done all the right things. I had trusted this person. He taught Sunday School for me. He gave out Holy Communion at church. He was the model member of our community. I still have a hard time feeling anger and expressing it. One of my sons who had been abused by him has the same mixed feelings about this man.

Richard: ONE is only one of the nine types. For a ONE, both the sin and its avoidance are the same word: anger. That's a special conflict we ONEs have. We're so ashamed of being angry. And we deaden that anger, even at a moment like that when she'd simply have to feel it. It's almost as if her anger would run away with her, and she knows that. So in moments of great stress, we ONEs close down because, like the EIGHTs, if we let the anger flow we're afraid of where it would go or what we'd do with it.

When I deal with ONEs in spiritual direction, I often give them the quote from John's Gospel where Jesus went into the temple and made a whip of cords. This is a great image of self-chosen, deliberate, conscious anger.

So I encourage ONEs, "We've got to focus and clarify and choose our anger, because it's our gift. We can't get rid of it."

When we leave it in this diffuse state we look for stupid containers, like cleaning the floor, instead of directing it at what really deserves our anger.

So, make a whip of cords, ONEs, and use your anger consciously and intentionally for good things.

9

TWOs

Using the same two questions, we will see how a TWO approaches stress and betrayal.

First TWO

My name is Joan. Just as sort of an aside, Richard says we "offered" to speak in front of the group. Two things came to me last evening when I was backing and forthing about whether I was willing to do this or not. The first was that I have a hard time saying no, and the second was a thing that struck me later. What went through my mind was, "Gee, people have been so nice to me here, I really ought to do this for them. This would help them out; they don't have anybody else."

Both are classic TWO thoughts, and they also reflect how I respond to stress.

I come from a nursing background and currently am in psychological work. I was thinking about the period I was involved in crisis nursing, when I supervised an emergency room for several years. When I was faced with a technical crisis and I simply had to do the work that was there, I remember getting into a state of almost deadly calm inside myself. While everybody else around was screaming or whatever, it was almost like, inside, I moved to this place of being so deeply peaceful, quiet, and calm that I could quickly do what needed to be done.

When I began thinking about the question of stress for this presentation, I was saying to myself, "Well, that state of calm was to get the work done." But what also strikes me now is that state of mind also had to do with helping to calm other people. My mental state had a calming effect on everybody else, and I was really tuned into everybody else's anxiety and their stresses.

In those kinds of situations, I could be pretty emotionless myself until it was over, and then later I'd have to do a lot of talking about it and expressing whatever had been going on at that time or what I found inside me.

Now the times I get called to crisis tend to be to more psychological kinds of crises — deaths and other difficult situations. In the first place, it is a real compliment to me to be called to a crisis. I'm delighted if someone needs and wants me to be there.

Several months ago, one of the doctors from Presbyterian Hospital was killed in a plane crash. Though I don't work for Presbyterian, I got a call asking me to come over and work with the staff. It was an enormous compliment to me to be asked. I needed to be needed to go and help.

When I get into a crisis situation, I feel like my anxiety shifts to the back burner. And when I go into an emergency room, I'm really aware of where everybody is who's involved with the event. I'm aware of who is in most need, the ones I need to go to first, what's going on with everybody else. And I'm not only aware of what's going on between me and the person I'm working with, but also of what's going on between them and the things I need to do to make the situation better.

That's always sort of at the root of it: How can I make it better? How can I help these people become more comfortable?

I don't like bad feelings among people or interactions that are hard to deal with. I always want to be the peacemaker, and I find in those kinds of interactions that I use touching to connect with them. I do the relational thing automatically. I put my arms around people, I reach out to them, I hold on to their hands or arms. That's part of my response to the crisis.

Again, later, I may find that I need to talk to somebody about it. I have found in situations like that that once I get out of the situation, then my own feelings and what the experience was like for me come to the fore. Then, I need to sit and cry about it or talk to someone about it, but it's emotional only when I move away from it.

One other thing about stress fits with needing to be needed. After the crisis is over, I need to know that I did well. I need to know that people were glad that I was there, that I helped in some way, that I touched people, or did whatever needed to be done.

In regard to betrayal, I think my immediate response is disbelief. "This just can't be happening," is what I tend to say. "We've had too good a relationship. There have been too many good things between us. I've given so much to this relationship that's been good, I wonder how this person can give back anything except what's good."

My immediate emotional reaction to betrayal is a feeling of enormous hurt, an internal personal kind of hurt that feels as though I have been cut to the quick. Anger may surface later, but the immediate reaction is always hurt. Even if the betrayal didn't have anything to do with me, I still read it as an attack on me, as if in some way

I had failed, or I didn't quite do things right, or didn't have the relationship I should have had.

The emotional hurt is always much stronger than the anger. Betrayal is like disrupting my world the way I know it. This brings bad feelings between me and another person, and I don't like bad feelings among people at all.

Long term, I think betrayal brings a real deep sense of loss and a lot of sadness. Maybe some anger, but lots of sadness. At the same time, I want so badly for the other person to come back and tell me that they realized how wrong they were, and that I was right, and that I've been only kind to them, and that I didn't deserve this.

What I've found in myself — this is more in the past; I've been working on this in some ways — is that I have so disliked bad feelings that when someone wronged me, even if I was not at fault, if that person didn't apologize, I would go back to the person and say, "I'm so sorry we had this disruption" or whatever. I would be almost ready to apologize for what that person did — just to get rid of the bad feelings.

Long term, I would continue trying to figure out "Why did this betrayal happen?" I would try to find an excuse for the other person, especially if they never did come back and recognize their own problem.

But there continues to be hurt. I continue to feel hurt that this sort of thing happened. In a way, something like this confirms the worst thing a person like me can hear, and that is, "You're not important," because as a TWO I need to know that you need me.

Second TWO

The need to be needed seems to me to be the theme of my life. Although I'm not in the helping professions now, up until three years ago I had been regularly involved in family situations where I needed to be needed. As I went from my family to families that needed nannies, I ended up in dysfunctional homes where there was one crisis after another. In crisis I was at my prime because they needed me. In those situations, I wanted to be helpful. For me the crisis situation became the primary focus of my life. It came before anything else — especially anything that had to do with my own needs. Everything, every focus was on that family in crisis and my needing to be needed.

And I was really good at it. I could pick up on how everyone was feeling and I identified all the dynamics. I was appreciated and I felt valued and loved.

When I realized that putting myself into dysfunctional families was unhealthy for me and decided to leave nanny work and do something else, it really was a crisis for me. I didn't feel I had an identity. I didn't know how to fulfill my own needs. I didn't know I had any needs except to be needed by other people. So I became very co-dependent and locked myself into a relationship.

So when I feel I'm not needed, I become really angry, but I don't show it. I become manipulative. I pull my love back and I become mischievous in that way.

I do really well in other people's crises because I know what to do, but in my own crisis I don't like people to come close to me. I need my independence. I need to feel safe with my vulnerability. I don't like feeling vulnerable, so I'll usually choose one person who I'll allow in, and then I just cling to that person.

And there is this horrible side of myself — that all of a sudden, I feel like I need their acceptance.

If I'm betrayed, I also feel very hurt, and I just don't understand it. I'm confused, because I feel like the love I'm giving is pure — although I must admit we TWOs are manipulative with our needing to feel wanted.

I usually won't verbalize my anger at betrayal, not for a long time, and sometimes I don't get over it. I hold on to it. My challenge is to realize that I do withhold my love until I work through it.

Third TWO

When there's a crisis situation in my life, I respond by taking charge of the situation and doing what needs to be done, because I know that if I do it, it will get done in the most loving, kind, and helpful way that could possibly be done. So I need to be in control and in charge.

In my immediate response to crisis, there is no emotional reaction visible on the outside and even to a great extent on the inside. I just close down. I shut off and don't respond to what's going on within me. I just keep the reactions all locked up inside, and I don't share them with anybody.

I tend to go to an extreme in this — I have in the past — I even stop praying and stop journaling, because I know instinctively that if I continue to pray and write in my journal all these emotions I have locked up will come out, and I don't want to deal with them. So I just shut down spiritually.

If it's a short-term crisis, that kind of response is okay for me. In a long-term crisis, however, I will often get physically sick. I came back here to New Mexico at the end of March for a week's rest because I had been in a four-month crisis and I most definitely was sick, on every level.

So it doesn't work to do that, but I still do it. When we TWOs get through the crisis (the stress of which is always very draining, of course, and requires a superhuman, saint/martyr response on my part to endure), I'm sure to let everybody know what I've done so I can receive all the appropriate applause, accolades, and sympathy. I want that sympathy.

My motto is that the squeaky wheel gets the oil, so I squeak a lot. I really want that applause. I realize it's not a good way to respond and I'm working on it, but this is what I do.

When someone betrays me, I am totally shocked. After I've given them all this "pure love" and cared for them and done all this wonderful stuff, how can they do this to me? The shock is usually almost overwhelming. It incapacitates me. But somewhere I developed the philosophy, "You might hurt me, but I'll be damned if you'll ever know that you did." And so, on the outside, most people never know that they've hurt me because seemingly I continue to function in such a way that even if they do betray me, I don't show it directly. I might not say, "Okay, do you still want to go out for hamburgers?" I might rather say, "Excuse me, we're vegetarian. Do you want to go out for a salad?"

That's what I do, and that's very, very unhealthy, of course. I mull over what they did in my mind again and again and again. And then I begin to plot my revenge: what am I going to do to make their life miserable? Of course, I don't do it, I just take joy in the planning.

In my imagined scenario, they will somehow come crawling back to me, admitting how wretched and miserable they were and what a wonderful loving person I am. It's a complete scenario. I know it well. I can't tell you how often I've done that and continue to do that.

I have a pattern of slowly severing the relationship — I don't do it quickly. If I just cut it off right now, they'd know something was wrong, but I don't want them to know anything is wrong, so I slowly become a little too busy, I call less frequently, we don't go out as often, and pretty soon it becomes a superficial relationship that eventually completely dries up.

There have been only two exceptions to this pattern in my life: a wonderful best friend for more than ten years and my husband. And that's because they don't let me do it. They recognize it. Of course, I fight them tooth and nail because I want to do it.

They're the only two, and I look back with great sadness on the relationships that I've ended because I wasn't willing to deal with my own pain.

Fourth TWO

I'm Dale. I'm a recovering TWO. I'll have to check to see who else is here from my Twelve Step group.

I was the token male in the TWO group last night. Voilà! Here I am. I'm blessed and cursed with being a TWO with a very strong ONE wing and a strong THREE wing. My responses will reflect all three numbers. If you think it's hard working on one number, try working on all three.

I handle stress two ways: one is public, one is private. Until recently I've been in administrative positions, high profile, and you better believe I'm going to look good under stress. In stress situations, I'm a picture of calm. I'll listen. I'll say, "Let's get this together." Things could all be collapsing, but I'm that pillar of strength in the middle of it all.

Privately, when I get in touch with what I'm feeling, the first thing I ask myself is, "Am I coming across right? Am I handling this right? Am I doing well?" Those are my anxieties.

As you know, the TWO has difficulty in identifying his real needs, what's going on underneath. Publicly, I'm smooth and professional and a-emotional, because I have to stay on top of things and get them running well.

If there's a sudden crisis, please call me. I'm wonderful in crisis situations. You can't flatter me more than to turn to me. And I will handle it fairly well. Of course, the biggest thing is that you called me. Thank you. I love that. It shows you have discriminating taste. [*Much laughter in the group*]

In betrayal, ditto, ditto, ditto to what the other TWOs have said. "How could I be so misunderstood? I've been so up front, so honest."

But when I'm at my best unredeemed self, you do hear about it. I go to my EIGHT point and I'm vicious. I will go for the jugular. You will feel the hurt because you hurt me. I'll let you know about it.

I've seen myself afterwards and I don't like it because I don't look very good at all. It's a whole other side of me I know is there, where I can be very sarcastic and I'm going to go right in where I know I can get your buttons going. Why? Because you dared to betray me and get on me.

Of course, long range, I can't handle the fact that you don't like me and I don't like you. So then I kick into my seductive and manipulative best to try to mend the relationship.

Crazy. Absolutely crazy. I'm learning that everybody doesn't have to like me and I don't have to like everybody. It's very freeing to come to that realization. But that's only a recent awareness that's making its way down inside a little bit.

Discussion

Richard: Did you notice the extraordinary articulateness of these four TWOs about inner states and relationships? They've got it far more than the rest of us. They understand the energies between people and within themselves. Young TWOs often don't, but these do.

Floor: I've heard in books and tapes that TWOs in their quiet moments sit and think that the people who have hurt you will crawl back to you and tell you, "Well, yes, you were right." Presumably, this doesn't happen. But if it did happen, how would you react?

First TWO: I'd be so delighted that I'd no longer hold anything against that person. It would be really easy for me to let go of any of the hurt. I'd be so pleased that this relationship would become joyous. It would be like "Kill the fatted calf." That sort of thing.

Second TWO: I agree. I would too. There's nothing I take greater pleasure in than forgiving. I *love* to forgive. But if you do something that makes me mad, forget it.

Third TWO: In my relationships with TWOs I've found frequently that they have the ability to get a lot of information — personal information, feeling information — from me, but when I ask them about their feelings to get personal information, it's like hitting a stone wall. Is that true for you?

TWO: Suppose we were going to have refreshments here and I could serve everything and people would start to say (provided they didn't know the Enneagram), "Isn't she loving, kind, and generous." In reality, I would have a brick wall in front of me ten feet high to see that nobody came near.

I give the impression of being open and honest and vulnerable, but what I'm really doing is extracting needed information so I can manipulate you to love me.

TWO: I can remember well when people were relating to me and someone would say, "What do you feel about this?" My response would begin, "Well, I *think....* " Some would catch me on that switch. I wouldn't use feeling words. I'd use thinking words. I'd tell you *about* my feelings rather than share my feelings.

Richard: That's the independence — not autonomy — that we see in many TWOs. On the one hand, they have found a way to protect their ground, yet on the other hand it's surprising that they're so sensitive to the world of relationships. But in a certain way they protect themselves behind thinking words. Well said.

Floor: As a physician I've come to value highly the TWO quality of the nurses that take care of patients. Physicians don't take care of patients; nurses do. I'm really disturbed by the recent trend in women of putting down the TWO quality — putting it off as pathologic, as co-dependent. How do you feel about that? Have you experienced that?

TWO: I went through a period of being ashamed of my motherly and wifely qualities and looked down on them. (I didn't know I was a TWO at the time.) I've been married twenty-six years, have two children and am a grandmother. I'm no longer ashamed of these qualities, but I went through a time of shame.

TWO: Probably because we hang out in similar places, I agree with what you say. I think this putting down of the softer qualities is an enormous danger. I think Nesbitt in *Megatrends* a few years ago talked about the high-tech/high-touch movement. He said that as we become more high-tech, we need the counterbalancing high-touch, which I feel is the caring quality you described and what we TWOs try to offer. But the high-touch is not valued nearly as much as the high-tech is in many instances, and I think we have to work hard to keep what we have to offer as a real value, as a humanizing factor in our high-tech society.

TWO: I think, too, it is helpful for the TWO to have a THREE wing because it can pull you out of that exclusively caring modality. The THREE wing helps me to feel more strength and gives me the ability to move back and forth between high-tech and high-touch.

Floor: How can you help someone whom you see moving toward disintegration or explosion of anger?

TWO: Touch.

TWO: Hold my hand.

TWO: Touch me.

Richard: I've heard many TWOs say that physical touch is extraordinarily helpful.

TWO: If someone can recognize that I'm getting near explosion and identify it for me, and just say, "Hey, Dale, what's the matter?" my response is, "Wow! Thank you. You care about me." It's just that simple touch. It all goes up in here. We TWOs need to share ourselves a lot. I am willing to do it. If someone will listen to me and share their ear, that will settle me down and diffuse my anger. I will be able to ventilate with that person because it's safer than dumping it on the person I was very angry with.

TWO: During discussions at lunch I had an awareness about myself as a TWO: how much I was fascinated by all the discussion and processing of all these feelings. What struck me as I went through my reactions to stress and betrayal was how important it is for a TWO to be able to pick up on your feelings, know what's going on in you, sense what's happening in your world. And therefore I'm aware now that if I'm really going to be empathic I have to know what it feels like to be a ONE, a THREE, a FOUR, etc. There is that sense in me of really tuning in more so that I don't miss out on what you may need from me.

Richard: That's a good way to end. Let's show the TWOs how much we appreciate them. [*Applause*]

10

THREEs

First THREE

I'm Tess. I took the question about stress to mean personal crisis, so that's what I'll address. I'm a physician and I deal with crisis a lot, and in those situations that don't directly affect me I do fine. I take charge and handle everything well. In a personal crisis, however, my first reaction is disbelief, and afterwards I don't like not to be liked. My response will be to look around and see if everyone agrees with me that it is a crisis (I'm relational), then try to stay cool and calm, and deal with the feelings later.

Speaking in front of a group like this is a kind of personal crisis, although THREEs usually do pretty well in public. We look around the group and can usually tell what people want to hear. "What can I say now that will sound right?" We do that well. I usually do that well. I can pick up on the group vibes, and I know this group is or is not going to be in touch with feelings. So I can say all the right things.

We THREEs are often accused of not being very perceiving nor looking into our depths, and that's probably true.

In terms of betrayal, the major ones for me have been relational. They have to do with loves or friends. My first reaction to betrayal is disbelief, but after that I have to go talk to the person. They're not going to get away with this. We're going to talk and talk and talk until we figure it out. They're not going to get away.

That's what I do, just talk. Most of the time I engage the mouth and talk, and that's how I think. That's the trouble, I think as I talk.

Like now. I don't have any notes and I don't know what I'm going to say until I get up here. Then I look around and figure it out.

With a betrayal, the first thing is, I gotta go to them and talk to them. I'm angry, yeah, and I can really be angry. And I can say that I'm angry and hurt. And I have to talk.

I don't know about getting even. I might play out some scenario in my mind. I certainly never would consider killing myself if my husband left me. I'd think about killing him, never myself. I might kill him and her, but never me.

Long term? I think this may be a redeemed THREE coming out in me. I think how I handled my major betrayal was talk, talk, talk, and finally worked it out. And then I come to forgiveness. For me, that's the key. I think the only way to come to forgiveness is to pray and relate, to ask God to give me that grace. I don't think I could do that in and of myself. I wouldn't have the strength.

Second THREE

I'm Dennis. I've studied the Enneagram a few years now and I think I'm pretty good at this.

I'm a sales manager, and a few weeks ago I had a major customer come to my office. At the time we were doing their annual report. When I arrived at the office, the sewers were backed up and the place smelled. Nobody was doing anything to solve the situation, so I became very, very busy. When a crisis occurs, I react behaviorally. I get busy. About an hour later I caught myself running around the press room — press to press — and I stopped and said to myself, "Dennis, what in the hell are you doing?"

I maneuvered myself back into my office, cooled down, got more centered, then went out into the press room and the crisis seemed to become a gift or a positive thing instead of something negative.

I can always tell when I'm nervous: I get busy. I can't sit still and I am not real within myself.

I like confrontations. I feed on them. I love to get people entangled.

I remember once at a family gathering I got the family into a big argument. I encouraged it. My dad is an old farmer, and he needed to say certain things to the family and I knew it down deep inside. All these family members were there, and I fed the confrontation. I gloated over it. After we got home my kids said, "Dad, you were having fun when everyone else was in crisis." I tend to do things like that.

Betrayal. I'm not sure I can relate to that. We're a Catholic family in Denver and we're in high regard and a lot of people know us. Our daughter is twenty years old, and a year ago she got pregnant. It devastated me. For about four hours. [*Laughter*] I got angry and said everything I could say. I just let it all go out of me. The family all came over, I had my day in court, and I just let it go. Then I softened. And I not only forgave her, but I also forgave her boyfriend. Forgiving him, however, took about a year.

Betrayal. If you don't like me, let's go out and talk about it. We can work this out. We can like each other if we'd just talk it through. We'd be okay if we'd just talk it through.

And I know that's what brought me to the forgiveness last year. Through talking, the situation just softened as the months went by, so I could take action. I could forgive.

Third THREE

My name is Jim. When I look at a crisis, I have to decide whether it is a crisis caused by my failure or what might be perceived as my failure, or whether its cause is external. In each case, my reaction is very different.

If it's caused by my failure — and I've just been through one of them — I feel broadsided. I feel destroyed, blown up. That lasts for about a minute, maybe five minutes. For a short time I want to run and hide. Then I get this feeling that I can find some deep opportunity in this failure. I immediately mobilize. I calm down and get clear in my thinking. I settle down. I'm able to integrate the input of other people, if it's a crisis at work or a family thing. I can take the best of all their ideas and intuitively put together a game plan. Then I do it. I've been through some remarkable problems that way.

I was president of a company until the first of May. Then I got fired. I was able to turn the crisis around inside me. By the 16th of June I had become CEO of a bigger company.

That's part of my failure, part of why I'm here: I've been too damned successful. I feel drawn to difficult problems. I relish them. Yet I don't like speaking in front of a group.

In betrayal, I've been very fortunate; I don't tend to remember betrayals.

Major betrayal. I have an adult son who's alcoholic. The betrayal I feel involves the lying and stealing that goes on in my house. Initially — I don't know how clear I can express this because the relationship is so close — I feel deep anger and hostility. I can verbalize those feelings very well to my wife; she's a ONE with a TWO wing. I did attempt to verbalize it to my son. We used to try and talk it out, but it doesn't do any good anymore. He's a SEVEN. [*Group laughter*] Maybe I want to be a SEVEN, too.

Then I start to rationalize the whole thing. Maybe he didn't steal the money. Maybe he *is* working. I start to put on rose-colored glasses.

Maybe I'm a failure as a parent, I don't know. That's another thing I think about.

Long term, I really gloss over feelings of betrayal. At work, I guess those are feelings I can't afford to encourage. Lots of times I think people have stabbed me in the back or not delivered on what they said they would, yet I remain friends with them. I know it confuses my enemies that I don't hold a grudge. I go forward.

In regard to my son, the counselor we were seeing kept calling me an enabler because I could forgive so much. I don't know whether that's a sign of a THREE or the sign of a parent.

Fourth THREE

I'm Dick. In handling stress, I shut down all my emotions because I know those emotions would get in the way of the solution. Then I figure out how I can take some sort of action.

Example: our last child died a few days after her birth. So my first question to the doctor was, "How soon can my wife travel?" We went out, bought a new vehicle, loaded up the boys, and went on a six-thousand-mile driving trip. I shut down my emotions and figured out some action I could take.

Betrayal: it follows a series of steps. First, tremendous hurt, even certain physical manifestations. It feels as though somebody threw a bowling ball and hit me with it right about the belt buckle. Then my eyes will have a tendency to swim. I don't want to get out of control so I have to get a grip on the physical responses.

The hurt is followed almost immediately by withdrawal. Get away from the source of the hurt. If the betrayal were to be something like an infidelity, it's, "So long, good-bye, adios."

Turn the other cheek? No way!

If it were something where I had less of an emotional involvement, say, some one did me dirt in a business situation, there'd be hurt and then there'd be an awful tendency to launch a torpedo midship at the betrayer.

Then, over a period of time, I'd feel guilt either for having launched the torpedo or even for having considered doing it.

After a very long time, a philosophical approach usually sets it. I might do some more high-level forgiving or rationalizing, but this step would come very late in the process.

Discussion

Richard: You can see that the THREEs are still relational people. They've found ways to stop the emotions from going too deeply, because those feelings will interfere with the task they've got to get done.

Notice their creativity in this. They keep the relationship, but they won't give you too much power over them, lest it interfere with what they're heading for. It's a masterful turning around of the relationship game.

This makes them good salespeople, for example. They are enough in touch with feelings to make meaningful contact with you but not so much as to let you hook them.

Consider how they related to betrayal compared to the TWOs. The TWOs couldn't really imagine how anyone could do this to them. The THREEs said, "I'm not going to let you hurt me." In fact, sometimes THREEs couldn't even remember a betrayal, which is their protection device.

Floor: How do you THREEs handle burnout?

THREE: I handle it by getting another challenge. I'm fifty years old and, as I look back on my life, it seems that about every five years I either change jobs or get a promotion.

THREE: I focus on something that's working, something successful at work or home that glosses over the rest of it.

THREE: I don't think I've ever been burned out. Probably it's because we THREEs never get so involved that we would burn out. I pull back, I change course, I do something, but I've never been burned out.

Richard: That's your gift. You THREEs are capable of having a lot of irons in the fire and holding them together there creatively. But the price you pay for it is a certain lack of depth. We all have our payoff, the way we survive. To maximize our gift, we minimize something else.

Floor: Now that you've identified yourself as THREEs and know that deceit is a part of it, how do you see deceit as it enters into your orientation. Can you see deceit as it enters into you? If you do, how do you deal with it?

THREE: In my orientation I can see obvious deceit — fraud, theft — easily. I have a difficult time seeing the more subtle deceit, and for a long time as I studied the Enneagram, I thought the experts were wrong. I believed I could sell you a car with a bad transmission, because it was your job to check it out. I could do that. [*Much laughter*]

THREE: I am reminded of a congressional hearing in which the members of the panel were getting all over the chairman of Del Monte Foods for what they thought was false labeling, because he was putting beautiful pictures of peaches on the cans of peaches. They said, "The picture is more beautiful than the contents." The chairman replied, "My God, what do you want us to do, make the pictures look ugly?"

I think that's part of the deceit. When I first heard the word "deceit," I rejected it because I instantly equated it with "dishonesty." Going back to the used car sales analogy, I see nothing wrong in washing the car and shining it. Now putting sawdust in the transmission, that's something else again. [*Much laughter*]

THREE: I'm in the printing business. I'm more interested in *you*. So if you don't notice the color's not so good on your job, big deal. That's no deceit on my part, as long as the result is okay with you. If it's okay with you, it's okay with me.

THREE: I think deceit is such is an ugly word that none of us would ever want to admit to being deceitful.

I think the form deceit takes in me is "never getting down into the meat of something." A good example: we recently completed our second trip to Medjugorie, which many of you may know about. I get so involved in the spiritual experience when I'm there that for months afterward I can pray, fast, confess, etc., with great devotion. Then my intensity just sort of peters out. I don't have the necessary stick-to-it-iveness. I don't know if that's deceit, or just my "Okay, what's next?" attitude. I hate that in me. I really hate it. It's my biggest fault and it's something important for me to work on.

Richard: You THREEs take on the images that are around you at the time. When the Medjugorie images are not around you, they lessen in influence. They move into the background.

You're right about your meaning of deceit. That lessening of influence you describe is not deceit as we formally use the word. But we have to use it to get you THREEs to open up to the manufacturing and maneuvering of images that you do, and to your believing of images too easily and too quickly.

Floor: How are you able to negotiate when you're angry?

THREE: It's simply a matter of controlling your emotion so you can accomplish your objective. If you need to negotiate a difficult situation at the office and you feel yourself getting angry, you're probably better able to stay in control in the work setting than, let's say, in a domestic situation. The reason is that at work you clearly see the objective. When the objective is clear, you have the energy to suppress any emotion that may get in the way of the objective.

THREE: I very much try to negotiate "nonfrontally." What I look for is a "win-win" solution to any problem. I treat negotiations as a game where I really work to resolve the situation so both sides win.

Richard: Winning is an idea that's worth addressing here. In other places I've pointed out how competitive you THREEs usually are. A lot of that competition is with yourselves. The game of competition is enjoyable for THREEs, but it doesn't mean necessarily to win over the other guy. The idea of win-win sounds good to them. They are much more focused on that energy of striving. For THREEs, it's just as satisfying to win by their own standards against themselves. It doesn't have to be a competitive sport, as long as it's a sport they're doing better at.

Floor: What number frustrates you the most?

THREE: An unredeemed THREE used car salesman. It really gets to me because I see myself.

THREE: Ditto. Plus an EIGHT. No hard feelings, EIGHTs, but we THREEs usually bump noses with you, because you guys want to run the show and we want to get it organized.

THREE: TWOs bother me the most because the unredeemed TWOs seem so needy. Some EIGHTs frustrate me sometimes.

I'd also like to respond to the thing about anger. It's funny what you said, Dan, about not liking THREEs, because it bothers me that you don't like THREEs. We THREEs want to be liked. So even in an angry situation I'll still do something to be liked, to come out looking good. I am probably a classic female, because in anger my first reaction is to cry, but in my professional position I can't do that very often, and so what I do is grow quiet so I don't cry. Later, after I've gotten over my need to cry, I can be very forceful. For a woman in business, the minute you cry, you lose. That has always made me so angry. Then again, why would I want to cry?

THREE: My big frustration is people who don't move or take action. I have a hard time with people who say, "Well, let's get some more information." To this I want to reply, "We don't need more information. Just go!"

Richard: The FIVEs are going to get to you!

Floor: Do you, especially the men, negotiate the same way in a personal relationship as you do in business situations?

THREE: For me, it's exactly the same in both. I have to win playing "Pup" with my thirteen-year-old boy. It's personally debilitating for me to play the wrong card and let someone else win.

THREE: I shoot basketball with my six-year-old grandson, and I think it is important he learn to lose once in a while. [*Much laughter*]

Floor: How do you THREEs handle failure?

THREE: What failure? I bug out. It may sound like a flip answer, but I pull away real fast. Assess the failure, then try to shine it up.

THREE: Six months before it happened, I knew I was going to get fired — it's in my journal. What I did was get mobilized. I looked at the weaknesses in the organization that caused it to happen; for example, I could sense the weakness in the guy who fired me — it was his fault. And I found a new organization that didn't have those weaknesses. I worked my butt off sixteen hours a day to find the right organization. God blessed me because I didn't have to move to another city to find it.

THREE: My solution is, as others have said, getting very busy.

I'm a sales manager, and when sales are down, I get busy. I call on more customers. I just rev up, bring my speed up another notch. I get busier.

THREE: Richard, I think you've mentioned that failure is what will bring us THREEs to our redeemed state. Now that I know that fact, my hope is that in dealing with failure it will point me toward God. Which is ultimately what we're all about. A moment ago, I said in a casual manner, "What failure?" And that's probably a true response. I don't seem to have a lot of failures in my life, but maybe that's because we THREEs can turn our failures into successes. God help me when I do. But maybe that's what we need and maybe that's what we should pray for.

Richard: We see THREEs in their roles: smooth, cool operators making it happen. What we also see when they reveal themselves at a deeper level is a kind of tender unsurety. Can you see this? THREEs are not the sleek, stainless steel, cool people they appear to be. Actually, there is a tender, needy, gentle heart at work in them, right below the surface.

I always take the time to look for that in THREEs, and it's almost always there. They appear to be completely free and independent, but they're more dependent than they look. That's what gives THREE a special kind of attractiveness, provided you're willing to get close to them. Now if you only know Dan as a used car salesman, you'd probably never see that tender part of him. When you get to know THREEs personally, it's almost always there.

Let's give them a hand for being a success.

11

FOURs

We'll give all of you FOURs a chance to make a fashion statement about stress and betrayal. We hope you won't disappoint us.

First FOUR

In situations of real stress I laugh nervously. If it's a gradual crisis, I often sublimate. I get really involved in what I'm doing, get lost in activity and try to avoid the situation, particularly if the situation requires me to deal with other people.

If it's a sudden crisis, the circuit breakers switch off and I concentrate on what needs to be done. I think I flip into one of the other Enneagram points. I work very hard at what needs to be done; I become really efficient and turn cold in the process. In a sudden crisis, emotions have no place, even though I'm driven by emotions in my life to a very large extent.

In terms of betrayal — I'm thinking back to a situation — it's very strange. In a sense, I felt a sort of freedom from the relationship when the betrayal happened. That feeling was a rather perverse happiness. I certainly went very cold inside. I probably had a delayed reaction. I withdrew but very much made up my mind immediately regarding the betrayal. It was the end of the relationship. I decided to go my own way.

I think the answer is that when I feel betrayed, I withdraw my emotions and essentially close the doors.

How do I react over the long term? The same.

Second FOUR

How do I react to stress? My business is stress-reduction! I remember once that recording tapes on the topic of stress turned out to be the most stressed experience that I had, because I just get overwhelmed with doing projects. I react to stress by feeling overwhelmed. I want simply to walk away from the situation, spend time by myself. I don't want to handle it, I don't want to go through the things that have to be done.

I also tend to be self-judgmental. I begin to think I'm not good enough, that I let things get out of control.

A lot of my stress comes from biting off more than I can chew. I consider that much of the stress in my life has to do with my work.

Crisis is another thing. To me, crisis has more to do with relationship than projects. I went through a bankruptcy once. That was stressful. It was terrible, but I got through it quicker than I would have a crisis in relationship.

A crisis almost blends in with betrayal. One crisis occurred when I lost one of my children. I can remember getting the phone call that my son was in an accident and was at the hospital. My heart started beating and I just got numb. I wished I didn't have to face it. I wished I could turn time back. Right now, I wish I didn't have to face telling this story to all of you. In crisis, there's a tendency in me to want to escape, run away. It's a period of denial.

What I tend to want to do is go to the beach, the mountains, or the desert, because I feel connected to God when I'm there. I immediately realize I need that kind of help. So I turn to God. I also cry a lot. I pretty much just succumb to my emotions about it, after I get past my numbness.

The next thing I do is reach out to people, because I know I need help. When I talk the crisis over with people, I usually come to the place where I can make plans and start to generate what I need to do to go forward from there.

There's a point in responding to a crisis where the energy really turns around for me and I am able do what I need to do to make it a positive experience for myself.

Betrayal. When my son died, I experienced it as a betrayal and I didn't even realize what I had done. I just realized it reading about the Enneagram last night. I felt betrayed that he took himself away from me. It took me quite a while to realize I was angry at him for that. I'm not good at expressing anger. I tend to blame myself. I thought, if I had done something differently, maybe this crisis wouldn't have happened.

I also see the conversion process in all of this for me. First, there's the feeling of intense hurt and betrayal — the pain of it — wanting not to see it but knowing I have to. Then there's an edge where I want to run away but I know I can't. Finally, there's also a part of me that wants to face the betrayal and move through it.

I always do get through it, but I forget that I ever got through anything else. I forget I ever made it through a crisis. But I always do pull through and I am always fine.

The quicker I go to the depths with it, the quicker I can come out on the other side of it.

Third FOUR

I also see stress and crisis as very different things. Stress is bothersome, it gets in the way of my joy, and I need to clean it up. If there happens to be one or two particular persons who cause me stress, I begin not liking them very much, because I see them as interrupting what I consider beauty or joy or contentment — whatever the environment is for me.

In a crisis, I react much more intensely. I tend to wear my emotions on my shirtsleeve. People tell me I'm an open book. In a true crisis, I go through an enormous basket of complex emotions. Initially, I can't stand pain. So I shut it out. I think, physically, I'm going to explode or die, because it hurts so much. So I first have to shut down in order to organize and get a grip on myself because, if I let myself feel the crisis, I won't survive it. So I have to back up. I have to take care of things.

An instance comes to mind. My father died very suddenly. I was in Alaska and my family was in Minnesota. I had to get to my family. That was the first order of business. As I was packing my suitcase, I couldn't allow myself to believe I was packing for a funeral. I had to shut down first. This was not happening to me yet. My husband almost had to do the packing for me because I refused to listen to him talk about the funeral. "That is not why we're going home," I told myself. I couldn't allow myself to hear it. My uncle, my father's brother, called and I just laughed on the telephone. People thought I was crazy. I had this incredible surge of emotions and I couldn't decide which one to select or which one to feel, because they were all so horrifying to me.

By the time I finally got to Minnesota, I was very organized and I took care of everybody else and made sure everything got done. But then I forgot to breathe. It was too scary for me, too scary to let go. Somehow, in that crisis I had to figure out how to transition that relationship with my father. I couldn't really let him die.

It was almost a year later when someone gave me permission to let him be dead. Physically he was gone, but I had to reintegrate him into my life. I couldn't live without that relationship. Actually, it was really healthy to bring that relationship back to a live sense.

So crisis is very hard on me. It is draining, painful. I feel it in my body, in my upper chest. I think that somehow my body is simply going to explode with it and disintegrate. I don't know how to put those pieces together, so I have to be very careful and allow myself to feel only what I can handle at the time. I need to assimilate the pieces carefully, very carefully. I need private time for that. I need to be alone, I need to isolate. I need to just kind of wallow in it.

But if that wallowing gets out of hand, it can be dangerous for me. I think about hurting myself. There's no logic to that, I know. Sometimes I need to think about hurting myself so I can feel the pain. Otherwise, the numbness comes full circle and I go numb again, so I have to remind myself to feel the pain. Then I get scared and go for help. I go to somebody and I tell them what's going on with me. If they don't understand the intensity of my pain, I don't know what to do. They don't understand and the intensity is very great. I have got to have someone help me get through that.

So crisis is no fun for me at all. I don't enjoy it.

Betrayal is not much fun for me either, but I handle it much better. I always assume people's lives are better for knowing me, so it seems really odd when they betray me. I make that assumption because as a FOUR I see such wonder and such beauty in the world and somehow I am able to incorporate that attitude into my life. Because of being around me people can share in that experience. And if they don't want to share it, to me it's like "What's wrong with you? Get it together!"

So if I'm betrayed and I've really had an investment in that relationship, I'll find a way of showing that person what pain is. My revenge comes in a very manipulative manner. I will appear so good that they will actually think that I had nothing to do with the revenge that has befallen them. They will perceive it simply as a consequence of their behavior that they have had to endure this pain or this horrible situation.

Then, when they come to tell me about it, I can say, "Oh, that's awful. That must feel terrible," when all the time I am aware that I have calculated the entire thing.

I'm not real proud of that, because somehow it usually comes back to haunt me. I have to give in and say, "Well, I kind of had a piece in this."

So I've learned not to do that anymore. I've learned to say to people, "You really pissed me off. Now we have to talk about it. We have to resolve it, because if we don't resolve it, I'm going to have to do *this* to you. [*Laughter*] And you don't want me to do that, so we need to get things out in the open."

My husband has been a wonderful catalyst in teaching me how to be up front with things and not come in the back door. But if I feel forced into a corner, I will still use the "back door" technique. At those times, the people won't even know what hit them And I'll be so nice about it. I'll really help them through their pain.

And inside my own mind I'll be saying, "See what it feels like?"

So that's how I deal with betrayal.

The betrayal I didn't know how to handle was when my father

died and I was real angry with God. I thought He'd betrayed me and I couldn't get back at Him.

It scared the life out of my husband that I was so angry with God — the things I was saying. I'm very expressive with my feelings and I also keep talking all the while I'm feeling and thinking and resolving. My husband did not like that. "Don't say these things, dear. Not out loud."

And yet that was how I got through the experience, because I was able to express these things. And I knew that the God I believed in could listen to me and still be there. So after the biggest betrayal of all, I have made friends with God again. It was a real interesting thing for me to do and it helped me grow.

Fourth FOUR

My name is Meira and I'm fairly new to the study of the Enneagram. Having been born and raised a Jew, when I found out I was a FOUR, I said, "Thank God, I'm still special." [*Much laughter*]

In stress and crisis, I fall apart. I cry easily; my behavior is like Nancy's. I feel like I'm going to explode and disintegrate. I feel like I won't be able to deal with life.

The feelings are so overwhelming, I call them my demons — the demons that rest on my shoulder. They just take over. There's no "me" left, it's just them. In times of crisis, they are the operative forces in my life, and it can be quite frightening.

I worked in a battered women's shelter for quite a while. Needless to say, there's quite a bit of crisis there. I was able to handle other people's crises really well. I was there for them and was very emotionally attuned to what they were going through.

As for a crisis in my own personal life, I'll be on the floor crawling like a little bug. Scared, scared of the overwhelming feelings that occur.

When I thought about the betrayal part of this question, the thought that stood out for me was sexual infidelity. I don't need two minutes to reflect on that. If you're gonna betray me, you're gonna die. So you'd better enjoy it. [*Laughter*]

Over the long term, I think forgiveness is the key I've had to understand for myself. I don't forget, I know that. But I can forgive.

Death of close friends has felt like a betrayal to me. It's been very difficult to integrate that experience into my life. I had to accept that, even though they were gone physically, they were still very much present in my heart and soul.

I have an altar at home, and the things that belonged to these people are on the altar. They serve to remind me that once in my life I was close to them and they are still there. They're there for me.

That has been an incredible lesson, because you do feel betrayed when you lose someone, especially unexpectedly. I have had to really work to integrate that experience.

Discussion

Richard: Here again, this time with FOURs, you recognize the tremendous sensitivity of the Heart space. These stories tell you the Enneagram has got to be true. But — let's see if I can say this right — we ONEs have a moralistic heaviness, while FOURs have what I call an aesthetic heaviness. That's still not the precise term.

FOURs carry a kind of laborious, burdensome weight. They see things with a tremendous sensitivity, but what they see best is the pain, the difficulty. They bring a sensitivity to a relationship or situation, but they tend to focus on the feelings that are hard and heavy. Their sensitivity combines with a perception of the tragedy and difficulty of things.

Floor: I've had a number of relationships with FOURs, and I always felt this heaviness and the depth of emotion, and I always wondered, "Is it real?" and "Do you really want me to understand you?"

And it's like they reply, "No, you'll never really understand." I get the feeling FOURs don't really want people to know them, because that might take away their specialness. That's the struggle I've had with FOURs. Maybe one of you might address that.

FOUR: I think I do want people to understand my intensity. I think I've longed for that since I was a little girl. Last night I said, as the group of us FOURs were sitting together, "How comforting it was that if one of us said something, the rest understood it." There were lots of other heads nodding "Yes."

I think, for myself, I am often in different mentalities. If I'm coming from my martyr attitude, I look at the other person and think, "Okay, just be that way." But when I'm being genuine, I really need to feel understood. Even if I believe someone really can't understand me, if they'll at least try, or if they'll just hold me while I experience my pain, it would be enough. Sometimes I don't need them to talk to me, but I need them to just be with me. So that energy of wanting to be understood is there.

FOUR: That's similar to what I was going to say. No matter how hard you try to understand me, you'll never really succeed because my emotions are so deep and so complex.

That has always been my cry to others throughout my life — try to understand me. Finally, I came to the place where I realized that there is no way that others will ever experience the depth of emotion the way I do.

Richard: That's rather universal in FOURs. They are one of the groups that like to gather together. A lot of us don't like to be with our own number. Others are probably trying to avoid going out to dinner tonight with people who have their same number. [*Much laughter*] But FOURs love being together; that's why we have these artists' colonies and Bohemian enclaves. What Nancy said is true. When she sat together with other FOURs, she began to realize, "Here are some other people with a depth of emotion who might understand me."

FOUR: Often the way I can get my feelings out is through poetry. I'll write it to you. That way I begin to get clear and it's clearer for you. It's a healing process for me when I write. In the depths of my despair, I've written my best poetry.

FOUR: I'd like to address that too. I agree with the statement on poetry. However, for me the struggle with the poetry is to make it slightly less cathartic and more general so it can be of some use to other people.

In terms of relationships, I think I've hungered for someone in life who would have an understanding of what was going on inside me. For years, I felt a terrible loneliness.

On the other hand, one of my issues — and maybe this isn't a FOUR issue but my own personal issue — is trust of other people. It is easy to let people just a little bit inside, but very, very hard to let someone in the whole way. I've only done it once. It's still not easy.

So, yes, if it's any help to you in understanding FOURness, I want someone to see my depth and to be able to go in. But it takes an enormous amount of faith and courage to let someone in; and if at any point it looked like they didn't understand or it was putting a big load on them or they might mess things up, let me tell you, I just run. You wouldn't see me for the dust.

FOUR: May I just add one thing to that? Not only do I like someone to share with me the depth of my sadness, but I also want someone to share my ecstasy. I have these two sides of me that are drastically different, and I try to bring them together in some middle ground, so other people can be around me and relate to me. But I am capable of this incredible sadness and this joy that is boundless. There are no words to describe it. So I have to share it through music or dance.

Floor: I'm struggling with your testimony because it is impacting me at such a deep emotional level. But one of the things I have a problem with is that I'm really afraid of my emotions. They're so deep. And sometimes it just paralyzes me. So most of my life I spend paralyzed. Betrayal paralyzes me.

Floor: Are you a FOUR, too?

Floor: Oh, God, yes! I don't connect at all with people up here in my mind. Instead, I feel this physical connection. But my fear of expressing my true emotions has almost estranged me from my family. I'm portrayed by them as very cold and distant. They can't understand why I'm so cold when everybody else is so warm and friendly. And I can't afford to do anything else, because if I let these emotions loose, I'll be out of control.

Richard: This inner conflict of FOURs is good for us to know, especially when we who are not FOURs think that these people are acting. We've got to learn to be honest with them and let them be honest with us. They really do feel things at a very deep level. They often have no choice but to move into metaphor, dance, music, and poetry as the only way to express their feelings, often because they feel we — those of us who aren't FOURs, who are linear, left-brained, or whatever we are — can't accept those feelings.

FOUR: I can really relate to that because I feel like I'm just going to explode. I keep coming back to my son's death because it was the most emotional time in my life. At the time, I latched onto a friend whom I asked to meet me at the hospital. There I just cried and felt like somebody pierced my heart with a probe that was so cold that when it was pulled out my flesh stuck to it. My solar plexus felt the same as when I gave birth to him. It felt as though I was giving birth to his death.

I feel pain in my body and, when I feel it, it's like I'm going to fall apart and nobody can handle it. I do know I need to express the pain or else I'm sure I'll die if I don't. I really physically feel as though I'll die if I don't.

Floor (a FOUR): You have every reason to be afraid because those emotions are really paralyzing and they really take you over. It's almost a schizophrenic kind of feeling, and often, even when I'm in the midst of this emotional intensity, I can still step back and say, "What is this person doing writhing on the floor? What is she doing?" And there I am, doing the whole number, both sides of the story. And it's really frightening.

But we're here as testimony. We've lived through it. We do come up on the other side. And we do learn from it, even though we move on to another series of emotional whatevers.

FOUR: The piece of me that wants to help you is the piece that says, "Even though it's really frightening, you don't have to do it by yourself. But do it. Go through the emotions."

If I hadn't lived through those emotions, I would be paralyzed today. I wouldn't be very healthy and I wouldn't have much hope. When those powerful feelings come upon me, I know there are certain people I have to have around me. But I also know I have to feel the emotions to get past them. And I also know I have to complete the path or I've left something undone. And I don't work well within my body if I've left something undone.

Richard: Thank you, all.

12

FIVEs

The FIVEs are now asked the same two questions as the other panels.

First FIVE

If I'm in a crisis situation with a group and I'm not the leader, then I find it fascinating. I find it energizing. At one level, I'm thinking, "Ain't it awful?" but at another level, "Ain't this wonderful?" All this time I'm analyzing the crisis and people's reaction to it. I quickly accumulate a lot of information, if anybody wants it [*Much laughter*] to help deal with the crisis.

If I'm the leader — and, as God would have it with her sense of humor, I've spent the last ten years in leadership positions — then my first line of defense is denial. Is there some way we can deny this is happening? If we can't, then quickly, if I'm in a group, we're going to analyze what's happening and then we're going to make a decision. We're going to deal with it.

In a personal crisis, denial is also my first reaction.

I used to be a very heavy smoker, and I always had a caffeine beverage in my hand. I also used to be much heavier. So I'm pretty sure those were ways I avoided crises and stress. I was sure there was some page or chapter in a book that had the information I needed that would help get me through the crisis.

In betrayal, my short-term and long-term response is the same: I immediately cut that person out of my life. I don't want reconciliation, I don't want understanding, I don't want to have anything more to do with that person or with that situation. If I can geographically avoid it, I do. And I have been using that response successfully for years with some relationships.

In the last step, if I must deal with the person, I deal with the person very superficially. Brusquely, but not unduly rudely. And only when it's strictly business. As soon as the business is over, then we have no more encounter.

In the last three or four months, I have come to realize how much pain that approach is causing me. So I'm tentatively opening the option that we might want to investigate other ways of dealing with that.

Over Christmas, I also read Charles Dickens's *A Christmas Carol* for the first time. I was, of course, reading it for the information, the social commentary. [*Laughter*] And then I realized I could grow old like Scrooge — emotionally isolated, self-sufficient, self-content. That was a little scary.

So we are very carefully reconsidering the old approach. [*Much laughter*]

Second FIVE

Hello, I'm Mark. For both of these questions — stress and betrayal — I avoid the situations. I just avoid the questions, at all costs. I simply would not get into a situation of real stress unless it was other people's stress.

Betrayal is not even something real for me. If it did happen — the times it has happened were times of new jobs and things like that — emotionally, I'd be pretty paralyzed, empty.

That's the thing about FIVEs: there is so much emptiness. To get in touch with feelings or emotions, you almost have to go to your SIX wing. Like with the FOUR — emotionally, I just stay stuck. It's like listening to sad music over and over. Or when fear hits me, it just keeps on going 'round and 'round in my head. I keep looking for ways of getting the situation back down where I can detach.

Behaviorally, I usually can't avoid stress in a work situation. I worked with kids, which was a real stretch for me, but I felt so isolated in my life that I felt pushed to take this job. As soon as I got on the unit, I discovered there was nowhere to hide. Fourteen kids, staff all over the place. For at least the first month, I found myself going to the bathroom and just saying to myself, "I'm going to make it, but I've got to spend some time in here just to get some peace." [*Laughter*]

The next thing I found myself doing was reading the paper, then taking notes on what was going on in the unit, then going home and reading. All the while just trying to get more information. Just going home and reading like crazy.

As far as betrayal goes, I'm so careful about this that I just take relationships real slowly.

I think back and ask myself, "When have I been betrayed?" Anytime I've really been betrayed it's been almost as much my fault as anybody else's, which is a FIVE's way of looking at things. In betrayal, I can even understand why the other person did what they did. If it happened, I'd probably be given to rationalizing what they did. Rationalizing whether it really happened or not, or denying it.

Emptiness. Long-term betrayal, I don't even know. It just doesn't happen that much because I go so slowly.

I guess betrayal means detaching in a bad way. It means just going apathetic until I can finally get to anger and then return to deal with the relationship.

Third FIVE

I'm Caroline. I agree with a lot of what both of you FIVEs have already said. My initial reaction to stress is to just get out of it. Run away. Withdraw.

If that's not possible, or if action is required — I'm a parent and I'm responsible a lot of times to respond to what my children are doing — the first thing I do is look to see if someone else will take care of it. If they don't, or they don't do it the way I think they should, then I'll try to take care of it quickly and efficiently without emotion. I'll be stoical while I'm taking care of the problem, and then I'll become emotional about it later.

I find that my emotions do surface, but not until after the fact, often at the end of the day, when I can be alone, when nothing else is going on, and there's nothing else to respond to. I've often been told that I appear organized, calm, and in control, but that's kind of a façade I keep up until I'm just with myself.

I also have the need to analyze and understand what happened. I also usually do that after the fact. I'll go home and find a book on the subject and try to understand more and more about what happened and what I could have done differently.

As far as betrayal, my initial reaction is that I'm really shocked. I just can't believe it happened. But at the same time I try to rationalize and understand it. If that doesn't work, then occasionally my emotions will erupt midstream. When that happens, I flip from being calm into being the opposite. My emotions will go out of control.

Most often, though, I'll just cut the friendship off if I'm betrayed. I'll have no interest in relating to that person, or I'll keep the relationship superficial.

Fourth FIVE

My name is Jim, and it's times like this when I really know that I'm a FIVE. In Richard's earlier descriptions of FIVEs, I remember him saying that, when a group of people began talking about feelings, he could identify FIVEs in the group because they were the individuals either sitting in the back or trying to slink out of the room. That's the overwhelming sense that I have when I begin addressing issues like this.

The first question was about real stress. I'm a physician, and I've been in emergency medicine for ten years. The first five of those were in a major trauma center in Texas. Eventually, I came to be the center's director. In retrospect, that seems paradoxical. The feedback I always got at the time was, "Aren't we lucky to have you?" and "How calm you are!" and "What a calm presence you bring to the emergency department."

In a sense, that's not unlike what Joan (a THREE) was saying when she worked in the emergency department, but for completely different reasons. She was picking up on the needs of the people around her, but I attribute my calm façade to this incredible need to try to run away and detach from what I'm seeing.

Clearly, the ability to run away isn't an option. That, in conjunction with not having access to the kinds of feelings those emergencies provoke in most people, really allows a FIVE to maintain this controlled presence.

Now, as far as immediate behavior in dealing with crisis, one of the humorous things I recognize about myself as a FIVE is that, when I'm going through the technical aspect of taking care of a problem, I'll find myself thinking, "You know, I haven't read about this particular problem recently. I think this is the way we still treat it."

We're not talking heart transplants here, we're talking about basic stuff. Everybody knows these procedures. I can turn to the right or the left and see that all my colleagues are doing them the same way. Yet I still have this question, "Maybe there's something new I haven't read about? Let me make a note to myself."

Every night I walk all around the emergency room with notes flying out of my pockets, notes listing all these things I need to read before I venture into the emergency room the next day. [*Much laughter*]

I do notice that, over time — years, perhaps — the reality of those crisis situations has started to surface, and I realize now that I now have more difficulty walking into an emergency room than I did ten years ago.

The second question was about betrayal. I discussed this question with my wife last night and I couldn't ever remember being betrayed. That brings up two things.

First, my colleagues are right: it is not true that I haven't been betrayed. Of course I have. But, second, it's difficult for me to identify it as a betrayal because I can always see the other's viewpoint. I say to myself, "Well, there are probably things going on here, things I've said and don't remember, or something in this situation that I'm not perceiving that the other person can see and knows and is therefore probably interpreting, probably in a logical way that's making him do this. Therefore, I can see that this action on his part is not a betrayal; it's understandable human behavior." That makes a lot of sense to me. [*Laughter*]

My wife pointed out an amazingly dramatic betrayal that occurred about fifteen years ago, and as soon as she recalled it, I said, "Of course, that was a betrayal. How could I not remember it?" At that time, however, I exhibited the classic unredeemed FIVE behavior, which was for me to retreat completely into the image of a person standing protected on the parapet of a castle, staring over the wall and not letting anything come close to me. After this betrayal, my retreat was complete and total. I was emotionally at the point where I could barely get myself to speak to a woman — any woman — for a year. For a whole year, I had nothing to say to a woman. After a year, I was eventually able to bring myself to insert myself into the normal course of social life. It had been an incredible retreat, hiding behind the wall of the FIVE. I think that betrayal shows the most typical behavior for me.

Discussion

Richard: Really excellent! That was a very good presentation of the FIVE energy. The rest of you can see the FIVEs' energy in their ability to compartmentalize, to dissociate, and to detach. They've made an art form out of it.

You also see the energy in their fine choice of words. Weren't they clear? You could easily understand them. They were struggling to verbalize their emotions, but when they brought them up, I felt like saying, "Yes! As a ONE, that's the best I've ever understood FIVEs. You are giving me the words to understand you."

Questions for them from the floor?

Floor: I was present at what I thought was a classic confrontation between a FIVE and a ONE. I figured it would be a crisis situation. The FIVE — I don't know how he did it, but he conquered the ONE by simply questioning and questioning. The ONE tried to answer all his questions but found it impossible. Do you find yourself questioning in these crisis situations?

FIVE: Questioning is the defense of the FIVE. I can turn anything in life around because I can be certain no one knows all the answers. It's so easy. FIVEs understand that. ONEs have the same need to know that we FIVEs do, but ONEs need to know so they can be right. The FIVE wants to know just to know, because he's avaricious for information. He wants to devour all this knowledge, but at some level he knows he's never going to possess it all. It's really easy for me, in any situation, to use questions in a hurtful way, because no one — and no ONE — can have all the answers.

FIVE: I would answer that question in another way. I'm certain that if I can get you — this ONE person, for example — to acknowledge my first premise as the correct first premise, then we'll no longer have a problem. Furthermore, as a FIVE, I am unwilling to let go of my first premise, and I will continue questioning you on your premises, humbly and modestly, trying to show you the logical flaw in your arguments. [*Much laughter*]

FIVE: I think questioning is such a powerful defense, that even when I as a FIVE get questions thrown at me, my first reaction is, "Why all these questions?" [*Laughter and applause*] Every time I get asked a question, I've got two or three questions I have to ask the questioner before I answer their question. This got me into so much trouble in school, because I needed to question the teachers to find out what they were really after with their questions. When this panel first got together last night, I thought, "I've got some questions I want to ask these FIVEs." [*Laughter*]

Floor: I'm married to a FIVE. What brings a FIVE to a relationship? Why do you need relationship? Obviously, relationship is what you need to be redeemed, but how do you ever figure that out?

FIVE: Pain. I'd say it's the pain of loneliness. Envy, if you have a FOUR wing. Or fear of being lonely, if you have a SIX wing. All those things.

The discovery of the need for relationship comes only eventually. It took me forever to reach out even a little bit. We FIVEs keep looking and reading. Finally, somewhere, the search for knowledge leads you to the fact that relationship is the most important thing in the world. When you're faced with this realization, it is painfully crushing. But at the same time, the knowledge will not let you just sit there with the pain.

FIVE: I think a FIVE can come to the establishment of relationship completely intellectually, just by looking around. I think that's the way everybody — or at least every FIVE — does it. I come to a relationship through my head, and why would I think anybody would do it otherwise? It's only after you get into a relationship that you realize that this is not just your perception of the relationship.

FIVE: Relationship? At times, I want an audience to share my information with. That's part of me. At times, I want people as sources of information for me. Then, believe it or not, there are times when I just want to feel cared for and validated and affirmed as a person. And even sometimes, I want to do that for other people.

Floor: How do you experience and express passion, either in relationship or in some activity you feel passionate about?

Richard: This is going to be hard for them. It may take a few minutes. [*Much, much laughter*]

FIVE: We recognized this phenomenon in our group last night. When we talked about passion, it was a real quiet part of the discussion. [*More laughter*]

I think this is really a core issue for a FIVE. For me, it was one of those breakthrough experiences to realize that passion took place in an emotional milieu, although I suppose you could become aware of this fact by reading a book about passion. I realize in my life I am never going to be present to passion in the same way or at the same time as others are. I will store the experience in my mind, and part of the task will be storing the reaction of the people with me. The passion will come over time — a week or a month later. It will percolate to the surface and I'll feel it and understand what that issue was. I might even be able to go back to those people later on and say, "Wasn't that great?" And a lot of times, they will reply, "What was great?" [*Laughter*] So, for me, there's an automatic time-delay factor to strong emotions, even to identify that there should be something passionate happening in a situation.

FIVE [*the following comment was delivered in a deadened monotone*]: I have that delayed reaction also. But what I want to say is that I feel passion. I feel that strong desire or emotion or force, however you want to define it, but I don't think other people see it in me. I feel it just as strongly as a more extroverted type might experience it, but I don't express it. It is there inside me, but we FIVEs are viewed by other people as not having it.

FIVE: I think the passion for FIVEs often comes out in something Richard has said about love. It happens when you get stuck out there in passion. "I'd rather think about anything than be stuck out there." But sometimes, by grace, I'm pushed into situations where I just can't do anything but get passionate. Which means, to actually do something, to actually be there. With me it happens sometimes with kids and sometimes with situations that seem unjust to me. Other times it happens in quiet friendship. There's something really passionate about just being with somebody quietly, and luckily I have at least one person who is that way.

Floor: I was wondering what numbers on the Enneagram you feel drawn to? And avoid?

FIVE: I feel drawn towards EIGHTs. I don't think it's because that's the number I'm supposed to go to. That's true, but I think it's really because they're so interesting. FIVEs like to watch, and it's fun to watch EIGHTs. [*Much laughter*]

I also like NINEs because they can be quiet and they're so peaceful. They don't like conflict and FIVEs have a lot of trouble with conflict. We're really vulnerable in conflict. I don't know where it comes from, but it's like we have nothing to defend ourselves with.

I also like SIXes. I didn't know how many SIXes I knew until I made a mental trip around my friends, especially old friends. I started to realize I love their loyalty. I can relate to their fears and I love their loyalty.

I think I have trouble with ONEs. I'm always afraid they're angry at me. I know they're going to be right.

FIVE: I tend to be drawn to the Gut-centered types, all of them, but especially ONEs. I think that's unusual for a FIVE. But I tend to get along well with them. I think it's particularly the spontaneousness of the Gut types I like, because I don't have it. I find it attractive.

I also have a lot of friends who are FOURs, and several who are SIXes.

I have the most difficulty with TWOs and THREEs, particularly TWOs. I feel like they're always trying to give me something I don't want. [*Laughter*] I need my space.

FIVE: I have only a ditto to contribute. I have my strongest attraction to ONEs — it's very clear to me. I like the way I can stand on the castle wall and they'll charge over it. I like that. They go toward what they perceive the truth to be. I can *define* the truth, but they'll *go* toward it.

I have trouble with TWOs. It's like if I want twelve inches between me and their face, they want only six, and I'm always backing up. [*Laughter*] In a book I read, someone defined a TWO as a Tootsie Roll in sequence, and that's how I see them. [*Much laughter*] They're so sweet.

Floor (FIVE): So far, I haven't been that curious about who's out there to have opinions about the different numbers, so as I try to think about it, I think EIGHTs attract me as they're putting into action some of the beliefs or convictions I hold.

Richard: Excellent. Thank you very much.

13

SIXes

Here are the SIXes. You should know that a public presentation is difficult for them. Give them all your encouragement and support. They've taken a risk and come up in front of everyone to answer the same questions about crisis and betrayal.

First SIX

I've written this all down so I wouldn't forget anything. [*Laughter*] First of all, in dealing with stress — you can hear it in my voice right now — my first response is to get very anxious. I might just withdraw. I often need to withdraw to think things through. I need to be secure in what my ideas are, what my thoughts are, and how I'm going to express them. It's very, very important to me that I can do that clearly for you.

Unfortunately, one of the things that happens when I withdraw to think is that I very often turn fantasy into fact. I have an overactive imagination and I'll have some paranoid thoughts, maybe catastrophize a little bit. Anyway, I'm liable to elaborate something so that what is not at all true has become true for me. In other words, I have somehow in my mind convinced myself that something that is not at all likely to happen is going to happen. I'm really good at that.

However, there are other stressful situations where I will take over immediately. I need to do that, too. As a matter of fact, I kind of put myself in situations like that.

I have taught behavior-disordered children for ten years. They are difficult to control. It's a difficult situation, but there's something about that situation where I mobilize myself, restore order and take control. That makes me feel safe.

So I handle stress both ways. I either withdraw and fantasize or immediately take over.

To handle long-term stress, I immerse myself in work. I am a cancer patient. I had breast cancer in 1987, and I dealt with it by not missing any work. My friends perceived me as very brave. I had chemotherapy, yet I was at work every day except for the surgery.

120

I worked hard, too, took on extra projects. It was very important for me to confront my fear and work with it.

Since then, when I have a fear of recurrence, I do the same thing. I have multiple things going. I teach a class, I take a class, I work, I lead a support group. I keep multiple things going all the time. So I guess one way to see it is that I overreact and freak out when I'm anticipating something stressful, but when the situation really happens I handle it quite calmly and well.

As far as betrayal goes, if someone has earned my trust and loyalty, which is not always an easy thing to do, I feel devastated if I'm betrayed. I may even feel like a martyr because giving my trust has been a difficult personal thing to do. Having given that trust and having it betrayed really devastates me. What I do in response is initially withdraw because the flood of emotion is too much for me to deal with. I become very inarticulate and I'm very emotional.

I don't like to deal with emotions, so what I do is write long, copious letters or write pages and pages in my journal, which allows me to release the emotions halfway.

I may not ever want to see that person again, but I will want them still to like me. I want to be remembered as being liked.

Example: when I was divorced, I helped my ex-husband set up his new apartment. I even bought him silverware at a garage sale because I kept the silverware from our house. I wanted him to have some.

Another example: I've had friends with whom I've had a falling out. If I find something I know will be of particular interest to them, I might mail it to them. I don't really want to continue a relationship with them or see them, but it's important to me that they like me.

I think that's where the trust issue comes in. It's not so much a trust of others; it's a trust of my own vulnerability. If I do trust someone, am I going to feel secure in that? Can I believe they will be there for me — that kind of thing.

Second SIX

I think for me stress comes in dealing with work. I usually cause the stress myself by finding other things I'd rather do than the actual task that needs to be done. But then, in the end, I work better under the stress. In stress, my shoulders go up, my neck gets tense. After the stress, I'll end up with a headache. That's what occurs physically.

When I'm in stress, people usually see me as having it all together. I don't show the outside world where my stress lies, especially in the smaller issues. Inside is where the turmoil is.

In sudden crisis, I separate emotions from task. A year ago in

June our best friend's son was killed in a climbing accident. At three in the morning, we were the first ones they called. I put my emotions aside and dealt with what needed to be done immediately. That continued through the crisis for several days.

After it's all over, I can allow myself to feel the emotions, but in the moment of crisis I immediately go into my head and process: "This is what they need. This is what has to be done."

Dennis shared about our daughter's pregnancy. When she had a miscarriage, the people where she was working reached him before they could reach me. Then they reached me. But before he got to pick her up from work, I had called the doctor, called her, and made all the hospital arrangements. He didn't even know where he was going.

In sudden crisis, that's the process I go through: organizing everything around me so everything that needs to happen will occur. I become very businesslike and can separate my emotions from the task that needs to be done.

Betrayal: I'll use our daughter again. I felt betrayed by her, not only in the whole issue of values where my husband felt the betrayal most, but also in the trust that we placed in her. I felt great anger inside, anger that could not afford to be expressed. I held it inside. As a SIX, you don't want to damage the relationship so badly that it can't be repaired, so you hold the anger inside.

Forgiveness does take place. But I think with a SIX, even though you can forgive, it is hard to forget. Large betrayals, small betrayals — it doesn't matter — you carry them forever. But forgiveness is there, even though it will take me a long time to rebuild the trust.

Third SIX

I'm Patrice. This afternoon I had an experience of what I do in crisis. We'd driven the car out for gas. As we were returning, there were no cars coming in either direction, so the driver proceeded to drive right out into the street. I exclaimed, "There's a red light." [*Laughter*]

That's a simple thing. I really believe that in most crises what I do is get very emotional at first. I may get excited and anxious, but I quickly step back from it and begin to plan a strategy. "How can I adjust to this? What can I plan so that the situation works out, so that I can fix it and so that everything will work out right?"

I may do my planning by withdrawing into solitude so I have some time to think, or by journaling so the anxiety becomes dissipated. The result is that I appear very calm and in control. That's how I deal with stress, particularly in the area of leadership or work or ministry.

I'm able to do better there than in my own personal life. About three weeks ago, my oldest brother suffered a TIA [Transient Is-chemic Attack] as I talked to him on the phone while I was in a conversation with him. It was like being in a dream where you reach out to grasp someone and you can't hold them. I panicked. I ran to one of the other staff members. I was out of breath. Then, shifting into my planning mode, I began to do things to enable me to fix it. I believed that if I could get on a plane early in the morning and fly to Phoenix, I would be able to help him. Through planning I was able to control the situation. So I became calm.

I really think I operate in two modes: one professionally, where I can quickly step back from my emotions, and the other in my personal life, where I often react with a great deal of emotion immediately.

How do I handle betrayal? My first impulse would be to grieve, to be very sad, probably cry. I weep easily. I'd feel anger at the dis-loyalty. "How could anyone be disloyal?" That's such an important value to me. Then I would put up a wall. The relationship would never be the same. I would promise myself I would never become vulnerable to that person again. I would be kind to that person and there would be a civil relationship, but in my heart it would never be the same.

An experience I had about twenty years ago of a disillusionment with authority was devastating because I had idealized an authority figure. When I found out that this authority figure, someone I worked with closely, had clay feet and betrayed me, it was devastating, but I never said a word. I no longer had any respect for that person; and I made up my mind, "That's your loss." I pitied the person; that's how I dealt with it.

Discussion

Richard: We've seen the gift of the SIXes reflected in the stories these people have told. We frequently use the word "control" in a negative sense, as in "He's a controlling person." But in a certain sense SIXes are good under stress precisely because they've learned the art of control. They can compartmentalize, put things in order, and plant their two feet firmly on the ground. They find themselves, and then they find out how to survive. That's a gift. They are the survivors. You can see it in their stories. Control is an art in a SIX when it's done well. Now, maybe the control need stems from an anxiety or fear, but it can be a gift. We all find situations in which we take control and we will survive. SIXes do it well.

Floor: I have a friend who is a SIX. She's in a relationship with a THREE. In relationships, when you feel the other person is moving at a slower pace than you, what do you do with your energy when that person is not moving as quickly as you'd like?

SIX: I think it works the opposite for me. I'm married to a THREE, and the energy level is much higher with Dennis than with me. He can push my buttons to where I shift into an unhealthy amount of movement and become frenzied with activity. I've had to learn to let him be who he is and allow myself to walk away from his energy so I can be myself.

SIX: In terms of working with NINEs, for example, that bugs me. I am impatient with them. Nothing happens with them, while I'm waiting to see things accomplished. I find it really requires a great deal of patience for me to work with NINEs.

I'm also a strong feeler besides being a SIX and loyal. I'm an intensely strong feeler — off the page. So I need to seek my truth as well as listen for the truth in others and that has become a real goal for me, something I challenge myself to, especially when I become very passionate about my values and my sense of loyalty, to step back and say, "Where is the truth?"

Richard: Thank you all very much. We appreciate it.

14

SEVENs

We'll end up with the happy SEVENs answering the two questions about crisis and betrayal.

First SEVEN

Richard arranged this so we'd end the conference on an upbeat. [*Laughter*] My name is Clark. It took me a long time to get in touch with any crises. I don't have any, because denial is the name of the game with me. Unless a situation is really serious, my motto is "Deny everything and keep moving."

One time that didn't work. I was driving on a highway at 65 mph and I lost control of my car. It spun around and ended up in a ditch on the other side of the highway. During the spin, I became clinical. I became intensely curious as to how this was to have a happy ending. [*Laughter*] I checked my seat belt, put my head back against the headrest, loosened my hands on the wheel so I wouldn't interfere with the natural course of events. The car turned around three-and-a-half times and stopped just before going into a large culvert, and I got out calmly. The only thing that changed was my state of consciousness.

The way I handle betrayal is to simply leave. I don't know about the other SEVENs, but I'm sort of a living *baklava* with lots and lots of layers — not that I'm sweet. If it happens that one layer of me is betrayed, I go to another layer.

I remember a young woman who callously disregarded my feelings after an intense four-year relationship. The intensity was apparently only on my part. She announced she was marrying this other person. I just walked away and left the relationship. The obsessive part of me recalled one phrase repeatedly, something I heard in an all-male context, "The way to forget a blonde is with a redhead." So that's what I did. I just walked away, cried for a while, and shared it with three or four important friends. I didn't see her again for fifteen years.

To deal with a betrayal, it's really important for me to put the event into words. I don't know about the other SEVENs, but I have to put it into words. I craft its story. I select the images. The images are very important. They contain and intensify my emotion, but they also make it clear.

So what happens is that any stress or betrayal moves up into my head and into poetry — images and stories.

My family intuitively understood my SEVENness and my need to shape events into stories. I once went to a party with my sister. When we got home, Mom asked my sister what happened at the party, and she said, "I don't know, Clark hasn't told the story yet."

Second SEVEN

I'm a SEVEN and my name is Joyce. [*Laughter*] What else? I didn't think about my name sounding so SEVENy until today, when it hit me.

The questions. Stress? Betrayal? I didn't write anything down last night. It didn't seem to be important then, but when I came to the session this morning and everybody had notes to talk from, I thought, "In order to make everything right, I'd better write something down." So I'll ignore it.

I'm new to the Enneagram. I haven't worked with my SEVENness, and I came to this conference wondering, "Am I really a SEVEN?" Last night I met with the other SEVENs, and I *am* a SEVEN. [*Laughter*] It almost seems a little trivial to be a SEVEN after some of the deep things we heard before now.

How do I react to situations of stress? I don't have any stress. I'm all right, so I don't have to face the stress.

Sudden crisis? I put it down somewhere deeply, as deeply as I can put it down.

As a new SEVEN, I'm just now dredging up hurts and tragedies I've experienced throughout my life, starting back when I was sixteen — that's a long time ago. I never could put them together even as a series of tragedies.

Just last week as I was talking to our rector, all of a sudden it occurred to me that in a period of four and a half years when I was a teenager, I lost an aunt, my father, my grandmother, and my husband. I never put them all together. Instead, everything was fine. Joyce smiled.

As I look back, I think I took pride in that smiling. I was allowing the situation to be a happy one, rather than a tragic one, which it would have been had I looked at it in another fashion.

Betrayed by a personal friend? I can't dredge that up. I'm sure it's there. Nobody can live as long as I have and not be betrayed. But I don't remember it. Yet. I'm sure I will, but right now I still choose to keep everything joyful and happy, and I'm not going to remember it yet.

Third SEVEN

I'm Rachel and I'm new to the Enneagram.

So, how do I react in stress situations? I guess I look for the bright side. I rationalize and look for the bright side. Usually, I shut down so there's not much emotion there.

I come from a pretty dysfunctional family, so I think during most of my life, until a couple of years ago, I dealt with stress through drugs and alcohol.

Under stress, I get a lot wittier, especially in a crisis. For example, ordinarily I can't even remember jokes. I either have to suggest, "Let's go out and do something fun," or get busy, "I think I'll do the dishes" — anything to get away from the intensity of the situation.

Betrayal? I think my loyal SIX wing steps in there. Betrayal is intense for me. So, in order for you not to know what's going on within me, I just have to shut down. I say to you, "I'm okay." This way, you don't have to know I'm hurt and I get to go on to the next thing. Then I decide not to ever speak to you again as well.

I think "avoidance."

My experience is that you caused me pain, why would I want to hang out with you? I'm going on to something more fun.

I guess most of my adult life is spent looking for the next fun thing to do.

Fourth SEVEN

My name is Raymond, and I'm a SEVEN, too. I didn't write anything down either.

I was thinking about this first question, "How do you handle stress or sudden crisis?" For me, it depends on whether the source is outside or inside me.

If it's a sudden crisis out there, my tendency is to step back and see if somebody does something about it. Suppose nobody does anything? Indecision and drifting is very hard for me to deal with, so I step in and take over. I come up with a solution.

It's much easier for me to handle that kind of a stressful situation than one inside me. If I'm struggling with something I don't understand, I can easily become paralyzed, even panicked.

One time, these inner struggles or conflicts reached a point where I realized I was seriously depressed, really clinically depressed. Imagine a seriously depressed SEVEN. [*Laughter*] It's angst in spades.

Maybe this is congruent with the way I handle outer stress. I said to myself, "Something has to be done." So I went and got professional help, and then struggled my way through it.

This morning something occurred to me as I heard other people speak, something that F. Scott Fitzgerald said, who was apparently seriously depressed once. He remarked, "In a real dark night of the soul, it's always three o'clock in the morning." It occurred to me that wherever we are on the Enneagram, wherever we find ourselves, God wakes us up at three o'clock in the morning, somewhere along the line. At that point, we can either choose to go back to sleep or to live at 3 a.m. for however long it lasts. That's doing the inner work, I guess.

Perhaps I handle inner and outer stress the same way; I just plunge into it and see my way through it.

Betrayal? My first reaction is not to believe it. "This can't be happening. It isn't so."

Not too long ago, I was working in a place where I just didn't see eye-to-eye with the people who were running the show. It had little to do with policy; it had to do with basic values, what I stood for, what my life should mean. I simply didn't agree with some of the things that were going on. And I knew that if I took a stand, I'd lose my job. I thought, "I have to do it, it's my integrity, it's the meaning I'm giving to my life." I felt somewhat like Martin Luther, who said, "Here I stand. God help me, I cannot do otherwise."

Nevertheless, I was very surprised at my own reaction when I finally did lose the job. I was angry. I felt betrayed. My self-esteem was really shattered. I thought, "Well, these feelings have something to teach me. I've gotta sit with them. I've gotta process them." So I sat with them, I thought about them, I mulled things over, and then I went out and bought a motorcycle! [*Laughter*] I did the only sensible thing. [*More laughter*]

A personal betrayal is different. It's like the unraveling of a friendship. For me, that's hard to deal with.

I recall one time in particular. My initial reaction was not to believe what was happening. "This isn't supposed to happen." I tried to patch things up, but it felt like I was broadcasting on Channel 5 and the other person was receiving on Channel 13. No meeting of minds. It became evident that this was the way it was going to go. The friendship was at an end, and there was nothing I could do about it.

And I went, without knowing anything about the Enneagram, right to the negative energy of the ONE. I became all the worst things a ONE could be. That's the way I was. I was judgmental, angry, passive-aggressive. It was not the way I like to be.

At that time I was reading a book by Paulo Friere called *Pedagogy of the Oppressed*. It was about how to deal with oppressive governments and it made an impact on me in this situation. Friere was against any violent overthrow of a government. Friere said, "If you go about an overthrow with anger, hostility, and hate in order to insure your own freedom, are you really that free? Or is there a danger of becoming the very thing you are trying to destroy?" I thought to myself, "That applies to this situation, too. I'm becoming the very thing I want to destroy."

So I had to take a stand, and gradually I worked my way back to the energy of the SEVEN.

Before I did my inner work, my joy as a SEVEN was rather superficial. It was mostly joking and laughing to avoid my and other people's pain. It was like water-skiing through life, just skimming the surface. But I hope, now, there is a clarity of vision I didn't have before. The task is more peaceful. My SEVENness still enables me to distance myself from my pain and other's, but it's an energy that springs up from the deep.

Discussion

Richard: Ray is a Franciscan Brother and, as you know, the path of joy is a unique Franciscan way. Somehow you learn to find the beauty in it all. But all you SEVENs have been good examples. Thank you. You all look younger than you probably are, and we're envious.

Floor: Why would a SEVEN ever come to an Enneagram workshop?

Richard: They usually make up the smallest number of participants, and I've given some Enneagram workshops where there's not a single SEVEN.

SEVEN: Let me give a SEVEN answer and then a more personal answer. I come out of intellectual curiosity, first of all. Why would you cure a neurosis of joy in order to go through pain? I, for one, am intensely intellectually curious. Secondly, I have four unrelated agendas here. I'm here to put out a newsletter on the Enneagram, I'm here to learn more about this material, I'm here on a pleasure trip with my wife, and I'm here to see my best friend. By the end of the day I'll have another agenda. [*Laughter*]

SEVEN: As I said before, I'm new to this. I came out of intellectual curiosity, too. I wanted to find out if I was really a SEVEN and why would I relate to FIVEs? I don't understand that either. I also came because maybe I didn't want to be a SEVEN. I never have liked Goody-Two-Shoes or Pollyannas or people who are always "up," for whom everything is always positive. I never thought I was that way, and it's just very recently that it hit me that I'm a SEVEN. I've tried most of my life to be a THREE. [*Laughter*]

Now I know why I wanted to be a THREE. It would please my mother, my husband, my children — and so it would bring me joy if I were the THREE they wanted me to be. I'm still not sure about my husband and I don't have my mother anymore, but my children like me better as a SEVEN.

SEVEN: I've been working with Twelve Step programs, so I've gone through a lot of pain this last couple years. I just wanted to know more about myself.

SEVEN: My first acquaintance with the Enneagram turned me off. A number of years ago, my initial reaction was that nothing true or good could be that good, that perfect. But I'm doing a ministry of spiritual direction and have found over the years that the Enneagram is extremely useful in understanding people and helping people understand themselves. Now I make every Enneagram workshop I possibly can.

Floor: As a ONE, can you help me in dealing with a SEVEN? I have a friend who is a SEVEN and really a pain for me. [*Laughter*] He'll call me at the office and want to go out for lunch and always has a lot of time; he wants to arrange my evening schedule because he says I work too hard and I need to get a little more joy out of life. [*Laughter*]

But I also feel sort of guilty because I do tend to manipulate him. I said, "I'm having a painting party in my basement — it needs to be painted." And I said, "You're pretty privileged because you're the only one invited." No kidding, he came at 7:30 in the morning and painted all day! And was happy about it! Joyous! I thought it was a drag. I don't like painting. Can you help me with a SEVEN who wants to claim me as a close friend with whom I don't wish to have a close friendship, necessarily. [*Much laughter*]

SEVEN: As an intellectual, I'd like to point out a psychiatric problem here. [*Laughter*] We have a name for paranoia when you think everybody hates you. We don't have a proper name for that *noia* in which you think everybody loves you! [*Laughter*] The SEVEN — this SEVEN — is more selfish than you may think. He may want what you may think is a close friendship. But he or she is in it for himself or herself more than you may think. However, if you're doing something interesting or new, say, painting your room, I will do it with you for as long as we can take pleasure in it. But be careful. I'm a sprinter. I'm not in it for the long haul. We can do a lot intensely, but then it finishes and I'm going on to something else. The intensity is real and you will experience it as real and so will I, and we will enjoy. Don't paint the rest of your house.

Another SEVEN: I endorse what Clark said. I wouldn't worry too much about the relationship because the SEVEN is finally going to find no joy in it and will move on to another task or another person. You'll be out of it.

SEVEN: That business of finding joy in things, sticking with it only as long as it gives some kind of pleasure, is an interesting characteristic of the SEVEN. This won't help you at all in your relationships, but I think of when I quit smoking. I no longer enjoyed it, so quitting was easy. I just stopped doing something I didn't enjoy. I've always said I hope I don't become an alcoholic because I enjoy drinking too much. I exercise a lot of discipline in drinking, making sure I don't get high, because I don't want to give it up. I don't want to give up something I enjoy.

SEVEN: I want to add one more thing about your friend. If I were he, I would be highly creative in finding new things to enjoy with you. For instance, I have an alcoholic son and the things that I have done to work with him would make a good story. I've done at least four things with alcoholics nobody else has ever thought of doing. SEVENs can't resist telling good stories, but I'm not going to.

The amount of creative energy that I have for discovering new things to solve old problems is really large. It's the same with your SEVEN friend. What you can get out of the relationship as a ONE is the inventiveness and newness and freshness the SEVEN can bring to you. The friendship can and will change frequently. If you don't like something he's saying or doing, tell him; he'll change it.

SEVEN: Here is one piece of advice that isn't as frivolous as it might seem. If you frown a lot, SEVENs don't like frowns. They react very negatively to facial expressions. Frowns will turn them off and send them away. Rapidly.

Richard: I think that's why we ONEs can turn you off. We can look so serious and moralistic. [*Laughter*] She's married to one. I wanted to say in response to Clark, that he centered in on something I haven't emphasized enough. If I could have chosen another description for SEVENs, it would have been the path of creativity. They can be immensely creative and imaginative and maneuverable in wonderful ways, even in dealing with something as painful as his alcoholic son. I could equally call the SEVEN path the path of creativity.

SEVEN: The metaphor I might choose to describe the SEVEN is being light on one's feet — agile. I want to introduce something that hasn't been talked about in the Enneagram: gender difference. I have an EIGHT wing and I'm not afraid of any man here. However, I'm unbelievably afraid of feminine anger. I can't face feminine anger at all.

Floor: Because you're very creative and tend to be good storytellers, what do you do internally when you catch yourself manipulating the truth?

SEVEN: I deny it. [*Laughter*] There is a resilience in me that if I keep pushing, I will come to a higher synthesis. I don't really believe much in the deceitfulness part. It's much more, "If I would go deeper I would see that truth is cone-shaped." I operate out of metaphors. I believe that the deeper we go, the closer we come to the truth and to each other. So I have this energy, and I will push you and share the push myself. I believe that if we'd just go deeper, we could get rid of the conflicts I don't like and we could come to a kind of unity. I think the SEVEN is saved by the FIVEs, and I love to talk to my FIVE friends. I just badger them, because they know they have the kind of depth I need to have for salvation.

SEVEN: I feel I don't so much manipulate the truth as much as embroider it. [*Laughter*] It's prettier that way.

SEVEN: If I'm telling a story for the sake of humor, to entertain people, poetic license is perfectly all right. Hyperbole is okay. If I'm expressing a truth that needs to be expressed accurately, I couldn't manipulate it. It wouldn't be in me. It would be a violation of myself. I'm not saying I'd tell it the way it is, because we all have our perception of reality, but I would tell it the way I see it. But telling a story at a party to be entertaining — that's different. I can embellish it all I want.

SEVEN: I would go one step further. Those people who are true but boring, [*Laughter*] I resent them. I think they do a disservice to the truth. [*Laughter*] I think truth and beauty are one and that you really only tell the truth when you tell it in such a way that you capture the imagination. I think that metaphor is really important: you "capture" through the imagination. The imagination has long been undervalued as a vehicle for the truth, but we SEVENs are remedying that.

Richard: Excellent. Thank you.

Part III

Discussion of the Types in Action

15

Playing Out Your Number

I feel it's important to put this entire Enneagram experience in the context of prayer and grace; otherwise we end up treating it as just another tool for "effectiveness," where the ego is in charge and we have to work it out, do it, manage it.

You can't manage the soul. The Enneagram speaks soul language, and you can't ego-manage the soul. I am not presenting this material simply to get you digging around in your psyche in order to change yourself.

One of the reasons I continue to teach the Enneagram is because there is so little technique to it beyond knowing it. To know it all the way through *is* the conversion. Grace is operating at that level. Surrendering comes with the knowing. It comes when you let go of the illusion, the lie, the false image of God.

At this point, I would like to open up a discussion. I invite anyone to make observations that you think would be helpful. For example, how did you see yourselves play out your numbers? Someone remarked yesterday, "If you had any doubt about the authenticity of the Enneagram, all you had to do was listen to those panels. You couldn't program people to be that predictable or that alike." Is there anything you wish to share?

The Numbers in Action

SEVEN: I'm representative of the SEVEN group. We really had fun as a group. [*Much laughter*] We did. We decided to have breakfast together this morning, because we all had already made plans for last evening. We had breakfast at the Sheraton. We told stories, we laughed, we were the center of attention of the whole coffee shop because we were making so much noise. [*Much laughter*]

We all had questions we were eager to ask one another. "How do you react in this kind of situation? What do you do in that case? What do you do when you get bored?" One of the things the SEVEN absolutely hates is boredom.

We talked about what we do in our minds, the little fantasies we play out, and what we do to keep our minds occupied when we have to sit in an unavoidable and boring situation.

One of the questions I asked our SEVEN group was, "If you were going to prepare your epitaph, what would you write on your tombstone?" The replies were wonderful. One of the men said that he is always saying, "What the heck, let's do it." So on his tombstone he wants written, "He did it." Others included: "Love is the answer." "It's been wonderful." "For all that has been, thanks. For all that will be, yes." "Thanks." "She touched the world in positive ways."

You could see that whenever one person would say something, everybody in the group would agree, "Yeah! That's right."

We talked about the movies we liked and we found that almost none of us liked to see movies like *Born on the Fourth of July.* We didn't like the hard movies. I go to them sometimes because my husband, who is a ONE, is dying to go to those movies. When I go with him, it's kind of like, "I took my medicine." [*Much laughter*] I was exposed to some of the pain, but we had a really good time.

TWO: Being a TWO, I can't do this alone, so I have to ask another TWO to stand up with me. The TWOs did not go out together last night either, because many of us had plans to spend time with friends, and we couldn't hurt them by telling them we wanted to do something else. So we opted to spend our time with our friends, though we were torn because we really wanted to spend time with everyone we liked so much in the TWO group. In the end, we went our individual ways.

Second TWO: The TWOs decided we'd like to leave you with a sweet remembrance of our presence among you. Will all the FIVEs please raise their hands. [*Amid gales of laughter, the TWOs pass out Tootsie Rolls to everyone, beginning with the FIVEs.*]

Richard: Actually, how you made your decision not to meet as a group makes sense. As TWOs, you would not have wanted to disappoint your friends here in the city to whom you had already promised dinner.

SIX: Being a SIX, I went to my group and, like everybody else, they had dinner plans with relatives and friends. After my sharing I said, "I need some 'happy,'" so I went to the SEVENs. [*Laughter*] But they had all gone out, and now they tell me they had breakfast together! Were they avoiding me?

Then I went to the FIVEs. Mark was the only one available. So we went to a bookstore [*Much laughter*] after we had a nice Mexican meal. I learned a lot about FIVEs in talking with him. That was important because right now I'm seeing a young lady who is a FIVE, and I'm wondering, "Boy, how do you tap into a FIVE?" Recently, I talked to another FIVE, and she was about as tough to get close to as the woman I'm seeing — or to get information from. Mark was very helpful in that regard. The exchange at the tables and the panels was quite revealing for me. It got to the heart of the matter. In the sharing there's even a greater depth. I feel fortunate I ended up with the FIVEs.

THREE: I'm speaking for the THREEs. Most of our group had other plans for the evening, because we've all been filling our time with side trips, so some went with family and friends and some went out to a party. Two of us were left. He said to me, "Let's go to Santa Fe (forty miles away) for dinner." I said, "I know just the place." We stopped talking, we made reservations — it was like Commando.

We made reservations at Pascual's, a classy restaurant, but since we had some time to kill, we did a little shopping. When we entered the restaurant, of course we had reservations. They treat people with reservations much better than customers who walk in off the street. They offered us a choice of three places to sit, a table for two or several tables for four. We took the table on the upper level, so we could watch everybody. Between us, we sort of jockeyed to see who would get the better seat to watch everybody else. We reviewed the menu and shared responsibilities in selecting the kinds of wines and foods we wanted to eat. We had to narrow our selections down.

On the way to Santa Fe, we had discussed how we buy cars, how we make decisions, the way we know visually how to get somewhere without necessarily using a map.

Among THREEs, there's always a concern about the best use of time and how to provide ourselves with pleasure along the way. For example, if before a business meeting you have an hour to kill, you might take a hike along the road, even in your business clothes.

We had a great evening and returned home on time. It was just perfect.

FOUR: I'm going to speak for the FOURs because I'm real envious of all these other groups. We didn't do anything, but I'm not sure we chose not to do anything. There were several people who said they couldn't attend, and as I was leaving I thought, "Why didn't anybody ask who could stay and meet?" Then I realized, although nobody asked "who could," I didn't take ownership of that responsibility either.

I wondered, "Well, why didn't I do that?" Then I realized that if I had said I could and everybody else said they couldn't, I would have been uncomfortable with that. So that was kind of how it ended. A kind of typical FOUR story.

Second FOUR: If I can add to that. It was interesting because we went back to the meeting room for the FOURs, and we didn't begin by talking about what we were going to do that evening. We started talking about feelings. We started talking about our struggles, our successes, how people have grown in one or other area. We were sharing a lot, and my sense is that we would have sat back there another hour or so if we hadn't had to leave the building and were forced to make a decision to go someplace else to continue. It was only then that it came out that a number of people had plans, so that ended our discussion. But when we first were in our meeting room, it didn't take us but a second to get involved with each other. It was the decision-making process that was awkward for us.

NINE: In typical NINE fashion, one of our NINEs had made other plans so Celeste and I were just kind of hanging out back here, with the room completely empty. We were pretty indecisive about what we were going to do anyway, just kind of waiting for somebody to invite us.

Lo and behold, our wing, the EIGHTs, invited us to join their group, which was very good. Just what we needed — to be invited. No hesitancy in decision-making. We sat back and watched them decide where to go to eat — and we joined them. [*Laughter*] Wherever it was, it was going to be fine. No problem.

The thing that was real interesting from my perspective was that I felt very much at home. The EIGHTs were very hospitable. I didn't feel overpowered by them, and yet there was a connectedness between us, even though they were just our wings.

There was also a FOUR with us that night, too. So if any of the EIGHTs or the FOUR would like to speak about that group in the restaurant, feel free. After that, we went over and joined the ONEs and talked to them, because they were in the same restaurant. So we got to see our other wing. [*Laughter*] It was nice to get that end of our number, too. We were pretty fulfilled by the end of the evening.

EIGHT: I'll just mention that John was the one who did all the inviting of the other numbers. In fact, I was waiting for him to pick up this microphone just now.

Last night, we had a very pleasant time together, probably in typical un-EIGHT fashion, talking to FOURs. As for the NINEs, it was more natural for us to visit with them.

All the EIGHTs didn't get together, simply because others had previous commitments or were extremely tired.

Richard: Was there anything that was typical of EIGHTs?

EIGHT. I'm trying to review the entire evening to see if there was anything particularly EIGHTish. I'd like a little help on that, John.

EIGHT (John): We were serious. No small talk. Not even about movies. Movies are just something that flicker. We wanted to talk about real life. Talk about these numbers and get to the truth. God help anyone who gets in the way of that truth.

ONE: Like good dutiful ONEs, we did go out and we did go to Little Anitas with the EIGHTs and the NINEs. After we got there, we spent much of our time trying to weed out a member of our group that we thought shouldn't have been there. [*Much laughter*]

Richard: ONEs have to do everything right. If it's not right, they can't rest until they fix it.

ONE: So we thought we had an impostor among us and we focused on that. After the meal ended, we spent about fifteen minutes trying to work the check out to the penny. [*Laughter*] I think that's typical of ONEs. That was our evening.

EIGHT: In light of this last comment, I just want to note that we EIGHTs took separate checks.

EIGHT: My daughter, the TWO, did not go out. I'm an EIGHT and I did not go out. My brother, the ONE, did not go out. So I was just asking them how we felt about all this.

I, the EIGHT, didn't feel any guilt at all. It's like I knew what I needed and I needed to get home.

My TWO daughter knew she was going home, but she waffled in and out, wondering, "Should I tell the group?" and "What should I say?" She went through a lot of "Am I going to hurt people's feelings?" and that sort of thing.

When I asked my ONE brother how he felt about it, he said he has a project going here, and he's only going to be here a few more days in my back yard. He said he was absolutely focused; the time after this workshop was for this project.

It was very interesting the way the three of us acted so typically.

FIVE: I guess I have to speak. We FIVEs all went separate ways. At first, everybody wanted to get together. It seemed like in the beginning we were almost going to get it together, and then, at the last second, everybody went different ways.

Luckily, a SIX came in, and he and I had a great time. After a day of being in my head, listening and taking it all in, it was great to go out and have some fun. I was a little intimidated, but once I got out there it was very good.

Different Numbers

Floor: During the course of the workshop, how many people found out they were different numbers than they thought?

Richard: I know at least one. I see five raised hands. Any comments? It might be helpful for the group to know how you came to a different insight in the course of the workshop.

ONE: I have read and read and read about the Enneagram but I've never been to a workshop where I could actually see the different types in action. I kept waffling back and forth between choosing the FOUR and the ONE. Anyway, I thought I was on that continuum somewhere.

When I was with the FOURs two nights ago, I could identify with a lot of things they were saying, but I didn't feel comfortable. I had a physical feeling of "This isn't quite right."

Then, when I saw the panel of ONEs I was sort of on the edge of my seat. And I knew immediately, just hearing them talk that I was a ONE. I could identify.

When I was reading the book, all the numbers seemed too extreme. I thought, "I'm not *that* perfectionistic" or "I'm not *that* hard of a worker." But then, you know, the ONE is always looking for the balance: "I could be this, I could be that." What made the difference was just seeing the people living their numbers right here in front of us.

Richard: Let me comment on that switch because it's not an uncommon mistake. You wouldn't think a FOUR and ONE would be confused, but here's the connection: Both ONEs and FOURs are looking for things done well.

For us ONEs, the drive is for the perfection of it; to see something sleek and clean just makes us ONEs feel wonderful. We delight in the perfection of it. But that delight in perfection can make us think we're FOURs, because we like things done well.

But the FOURs like things done well with a very different energy. It's not the perfection of it, it's the class of it they like, the taste of it, the style of it.

Both responses to things done well look the same, but they're really not. That's why there's an arrow between the two numbers. It's not uncommon for ONEs to think they're FOURs and vice versa, although not as common in the vice versa direction.

SEVEN: I've been studying the Enneagram for about six years. When I initially learned it, I thought I was a SEVEN. I felt I was a SEVEN. And then when I went through a bout with cancer, it threw me back into the court of fear and I began to think I was a SIX. But yesterday was so definitive for me, because I could spend time with SIXes *and* SEVENs.

I discovered there was something about the SIXes that was too heavy for me. It was just too heavy. I felt the heaviness almost as a physical response.

Being with the SEVENs was kind of lighter; it's where I like to be. Now, when I think back on how I dealt with the cancer, I realize I did it very positively. I did positive things. I went into my FIVEness and read everything I could about cancer. It was like *knowing* was going to keep me safe. I kept doing positive things all the way through the treatment.

It just felt better as I thought about SEVENness. Spending time with them at breakfast this morning, I thought, "Yes, I'm a SEVEN."

It feels good. [*Laughter*] I feel real positive about that and I like feeling positive.

Richard: I think she's got the right number. Remember she was on the SIX panel, and her energy wasn't completely in sync with the others. [*I invite the reader to review the chapter on the SIXes and see if you can identify Dorothy as a SEVEN among the SIXes.*]

FIVE: I'm new at the Enneagram and had read the book before I came here. That was really the extent of it. I'm a psychologist and felt sure I was a TWO because I spend a lot of time counseling people in relationships. However, I'm also fifty years old and have never been married and feel empty all the time — with my doctorate and all kinds of training. So I believe I'm a FIVE just now getting in touch with emotions. It's hard to go from the heart to the head, but it really fits now. I can acknowledge my need to retreat.

At first, I joined the TWO group here because I thought I fitted in with the TWOs, but I think they discerned right away that I wasn't a sister. [*Laughter*]

I now really feel comfortable with the FIVEs and am working from within that number.

Richard: I'm really glad you shared that with us because you'd never think TWOs and FIVEs could be confused, and here's obviously a woman who's educated, knows herself, and still confused the two numbers.

She is probably a good example of how women in particular take on a *persona* that's not their true *persona*. You were in a helping profession besides, but undoubtedly as a true FIVE you've paid a heavy price for that — living out a self-image of a helper when in fact — look at her — she's the polar opposite.

I always call TWOs compulsive givers and FIVEs compulsive takers. It sounds like a negative judgment but I don't mean it that way. I mean it in terms of energy movement, the direction of energy flow.

I hope this new awareness of your FIVEness is going to give you a tremendous freedom to love yourself. I hope it gives you all kinds of permissions to trust the quiet space you need and want and not feel you have to apologize for it.

FIVE's Response: There have been conflicts. I could feel myself wanting mysticism and could feel myself being attracted and led that way, but then I'd pull back. Yes, there have been a lot of inner conflicts that can now be resolved. [*Applause*]

Richard: That's wonderful.

Floor: You know me, Richard.

Richard: You're not anything but a NINE, are you?

NINE: I'm going to say something very profound. [*Laughter*] An interesting observation Mary and I made — we are really new acquaintances. Coming here, we discovered we're both NINEs and we're both Cancers. Cancer is the crab that holds on. But the joke is I didn't recognize my holding on. In the course of our conversation, I revealed that I'm recently divorced after forty-four years of marriage. And she said to me, "No wonder it took you forty-three years to make up your mind. You're a NINE!" [*Much laughter*]

Richard: That's great. Thank you.

16

Being True to Yourself

Living the Wrong Number

Question from the Floor: To any of the people who thought they were a number other than the one they've since discovered they are: "Did you have any physical manifestations, such as illnesses, that went hand in hand with living the wrong number? Forcing your energy? The square peg in the round hole?"

The New FIVE: Well, I'm aware that a lot of times I got sick in order to retreat. Sickness was my friend; it helped me to get away. I think getting sick was my comfort. It was my way of getting to my FIVE.

Yes, it's interesting, now that I think of it. I could work during the week, but I got sick every weekend. I began noticing that pattern in my health but couldn't figure it out. Now I can see the conflict of the social expectations and my own desire to be alone and retreat.

Richard: She thought she was a TWO, but by getting sick, she got the time off her FIVE energy needed. An excellent example.

You can't be something other than who you are! You'll pay a price for trying. You'll suffer and the body will show it.

A New SEVEN: My digestive system is shot because I was always trying to do things I couldn't do.

Richard: On the panels, you thought you were a THREE. But you realized you were a SEVEN.

EIGHT: I'm an EIGHT, but I think from being in high school during the 1950s and growing up through twelve years of Catholic education — until I was about twenty-six or twenty-seven — I behaved something like a ONE or a TWO or somewhere in between. This is the truth: During my entire life up until that time, I'd struggled with stomach aches, severe stomach aches. Then, once I got into activism and really became myself by letting some of the passion out, the stomach aches absolutely disappeared.

Richard: There's an example of a "bad girl" trying to play the "good girl" role, and she got sick pushing down whole bunches of her necessary bad-girl energy in trying to be a good girl. You're NOT a good girl! [*Much laughter*]

EIGHT (*addressing her daughter*): Forgive me. You know!

Richard: This is her daughter, Maureen, who *is* a "good girl."
[*Laughter*]

EIGHT: Most of the time [*the mother commenting on her daughter*]. As a TWO during much of my life, I always had stomach problems until I decided to go off to Taos and be a ski bum and focus on my own life. Then the stomach problems vanished. In striving for that balance, I feel healthier physically.

Richard: She focused on her own needs, which is what a TWO finds it hard to do. Before that, she was always meeting everybody else's needs, and she had stomach problems. With the switch to "I'm going to do what I want to do" — work at a ski shop in Taos — her stomach problems vanished.

I see the SEVENs want to go with you to the ski resort! [*Laughter*]

FOUR: I just wanted to share the fact that I discovered my FOUR-ness through my dreams. I don't know if anybody else ever did that. I practiced law for years and was very unhappy with it. I had nightmares; one nightmare in particular cracks me up today when I think about it. In the dream, I was standing in line for a very tacky yard sale. [*Laughter*]

When I got up to the yard sale, this very humble little Asian monk offered me the opportunity to rake his yard. Next thing I knew, I was out there raking his yard and feeling very good about it.

Richard: Wow! That's really neat.

SEVEN: I recall something that's pretty indicative of my SEVEN-ness. I did a lot of thinking after I was diagnosed with cancer in 1987. At the time, I only suspected it was SEVEN energy. Now my behavior is making more sense to me, and I'm sure of it. For me as a SEVEN, it's really important to have a future, to have a goal, to have a plan, to have something to look forward to. Around the time just before the cancer was diagnosed, I remember coming back on the train from Chicago to Albuquerque having an image of this big black feeling or big black pot on my chest. At the time, I didn't have a goal or a future. I was feeling really in a rut. I was stagnant. Life felt so, so uncomfortable. I didn't have something to grab on to or anything to look forward to. That was in August, and in September a mammogram showed that I had breast cancer.

As I reflected about it over time, I think that connection was really significant for me, especially now that I'm feeling comfortable with my SEVENness. It is so important for SEVENs to have a positive future goal. It's such an important part of their life that if they don't have that, there's a real emptiness. Real bad feeling.

I don't want to say that not having a goal or a future caused my illness, but I think it had some effect on the way I thought through things. Now I make sure I have a goal. I'm going to be an art therapist. That's a really concrete goal that I'm working toward now.

Richard: You can see why death is just such an impossible notion for a SEVEN. In a certain sense, apart from faith, death offers no future positive goal. Death means you just lose your energy. My father is eighty-one now and he can't speak of death, even though he's eighty-one. As a SEVEN, death is unthinkable.

Floor: As an Enneagram team workshop leader, one of the things we have discovered is a way of working with people who are unsure as to what their number is. When they're unsure, we ask them, "What's your first reaction in a situation?" We ask them to notice whether they begin thinking about it (mind), or feeling it in physical manifestations (gut), or do their emotions immediately get involved (heart).

Once they can locate themselves in one of the centers, they've reduced their alternatives to three. If they can pinpoint the center from which they operate, then it's just a matter of isolating one of the three numbers in that center.

Also a flip-flop between centers probably indicates their wings, either from the heart to the head or the gut to the heart. That simple question — to pinpoint the center — has been helpful in a lot of instances.

FOUR: As a child I grew up in a fundamentalist religion. Every Saturday when we went to church, I developed a stomach ache. The discussion we've been having just reminded me of it. I would have a stomach ache all day, because I was being taught something that wasn't authentic to me.

FOURs need to be authentic. As a child I wasn't allowed to create my own path, to find my own way.

I was just thinking about all the children that have things forced on them and aren't allowed their own way. How wonderful it would be if parents could know something about the Enneagram when they are raising their children. They would be receptive to the child's special path and support it.

The Enneagram and Parenting

Richard: I would think that the Enneagram could be a great help in parenting.

SEVEN: Thinking back on it, I lived sort of an ambivalent life. I was a SEVEN outside the house and a THREE at home. Physically and psychologically, it was very destructive.

Richard: At least you were able to dance between the worlds of those two numbers. That kept your sanity. You didn't have permission to be a SEVEN at home. Families generally don't give such permission. Perhaps that's why we use the word "dysfunctional" family. We're given a script within the family, and sometimes it's not our script.

FOUR: I can attest to that. We have a FOUR daughter, and we've known her number for a long time. We give Enneagram workshops in Denver; we've done it for about six years with families and couples. Our FOUR daughter, who's now nineteen, had her head shaved on the side. She went to Goodwill Industries to buy her clothes. She would walk out of the house looking like who knows what — and you'd wonder. But we knew she was a FOUR and we supported her. We prayed her through high school. She did well. She's really a neat lady, and we just stayed with her. We had neighborhood comments like, "How could these people allow their child to look like this?"

Our daughter went to the missions in Chile three months ago. She works at an orphanage there. Her letters to us are unbelievable. She's growing in wonderful ways. She's getting in touch with her isolation and her desolation. She's quoting Henri Nouwen. I didn't even know who he was. Every letter that comes reflects her new-found depth.

About two month before she left for Chile, she told my wife, "All these years, I've had my bags packed, if you guys began to fight me on who I was."

We didn't, and now she's blossomed.

Richard: That's a wonderful example of wise parenting.

FOUR: I grew up in a military family. In that family, everything was "what you did" — the task. No one was ever interested in "who you were" — in "being." And I'm a FOUR who lived all my life as a THREE because that was something I could do that was acceptable.

I remember being told by my family, "Come back and live in the real world. Don't be a dreamer." All the while, I had little fantasy playmates and an imaginary world that I retreated into.

It's so freeing just to be yourself.

My husband is a THREE and he does not like to deal with anything deep at all, whereas that's all I want to deal with. So it's a help to realize that it is okay to work on getting to God because you get yourself out of the way.

SIX: I'm her SIX daughter and we'd like to rent a FOUR daughter to come live with us, please! [*Much laughter*]

TWO: I was thinking about a comment Richard made at the beginning, how sometime early in life he chose to be a ONE. Well, I grew up in a household where the message I got was that I would be loved only if I was a good little boy. So I chose to be a TWO and bought right into that number. I was not only a good little boy, I was disgustingly Goody-Two-Shoes.

But privately, I was very bad. My badness couldn't be public lest people might not like me, accept me, or give me what I needed. Privately, I have been a bad little boy throughout the first forty-eight years of my life.

The Enneagram, to which I was introduced a year or so ago, was a very freeing experience for me. I could actually ask myself, "What do I want?" That was a brand new question. It had never occurred to me.

I know now that what I had been doing on the bad side all my life was answering that question. I was doing what I really wanted to do, but I couldn't acknowledge that.

Even though I found the Enneagram very freeing, I still came to it with a forty-eight-year-old tape playing in my mind. I've done only a year-and-a-half of work on the Enneagram; it still takes a little bit of time.

I remember the first time I asked myself, "What are my needs?" I didn't have the foggiest notion, which again confirmed the TWO pretty accurately.

Being What You Are

Richard: For some reason, it's good for people to see men who are TWOs because we most often associate that number with the feminine. I appreciate your speaking.

I faced the same dilemma, probably in my own way. I have such a strong TWO wing that when I first identified it twenty years ago I went back and forth for quite a while, not sure whether I was a ONE or a TWO.

ONEs and TWOs often go back and forth a long time. That's not an uncommon dilemma because both numbers are seeking something outside of themselves: we ONEs are seeking a *principle* to tell us what to do; the TWOs are seeking a *person* to tell them what to do. Even so, I'm not quite sure whether it's primarily a principle that guides me or a person's wishes for me. I've seen people go for years unable to decide what it is that finally pushes them, people or principles.

This dilemma is very common for people in religion. ONE-TWO people are guided, on the one hand, by the servant/martyr profile of the TWO of Jesus: put yourself on the cross and offer yourself as a servant to the world; and, on the other hand, the ONE of Jesus: the laws and the principles and ideals of religion. There's a lot of us riding on the horns of that dilemma.

SIX: One day about three years ago, I remember my spiritual director saying, "What is it that you really, really want?" And I sat there for a long time and then said, "Father, I can't think of anything."

Is that a problem of the SIX?

Richard: Let's speak to that. The TWO and the SIX are another pair commonly confused, and you're naming the problem well.

All through your life as a SIX, you have guided yourself by law, principle, authority, guidelines from outside yourself. And so when someone comes up to you in the middle of life and asks you what you really want — or as we used to say in spiritual direction, "What is your true heart's desire?" — TWOs and SIXes in particular do not know what you are talking about.

That's very common among SIXes. That's why we have to urge you SIXes to develop inner authority. We encourage SIXes, "Do something that's purely self-starting, self-initiated from within. You will feel guilty at first, but do it."

Now, this hesitancy and guilt may be true of all numbers at first. In this very conversation, for example, don't most of you notice a twinge of guilt? Aren't you asking yourself something like, "How dare I be true to myself? Isn't that pure selfishness? Isn't that going to get me into individualism?"

Of course, it could go the selfish route, but that's not what we're talking about. We're talking about a necessary starting point in spiritual growth. That's what I meant when I said about creation already being redemption: Creation is God telling us who we are in our very being, and it's the necessary starting point of your path. It's the redemptive starting point. It has to be.

I think that's why we have so much distorted and unhappy religion today. People have used something other than their own creation — their own being — as the necessary starting point.

A common starting point is idealism. But idealism is normally a love of ideals, rather than love of what is. Idealism tells us to be what we ought to be (and who defines that?) rather than to be what we are.

What God has allowed is the love of what is.

However, for many of us that transfer from the love of ideals to the love of what is, for some reason, gets accompanied by guilt.

I know if I were a parent, the way of ideals would seem to me to be the only way to keep the kids in order. Suppose you're a FIVE or SIX or even a TWO. You have to keep some order in the house. You say to your children, "You can't do that and you can't be that way because I have to exist through the day in this house just as much as you do."

So what else can parents do?

There's no point in blaming parents. America has been into blaming parents for fifteen years now. Everything now is blame parents for whatever is wrong with you. The church had a name for this situation of inheriting the parental wounds; it was called original sin. The church assured us that everybody had original sin. Everybody. In a very theologically simple way, the church always taught that these wounds are necessarily passed down to you through your parents.

We call baptism the healing of original sin. To enter into the great mystery of God's love, which is what baptism should symbolize, is the only way to heal the parental wound.

Don't hate your parents for giving you your woundedness. They have to give it. They can't avoid giving it. And remember, you're going to be a parent too. You're going to pass on to your children some of your unlived life, some of your mistakenness, some of your compulsiveness. I don't care how many Enneagram workshops you take and how healed and whole you are, you will pass on some of your unwholeness to your children. That's your finitude. Courage is to accept that we are finite.

We have to take responsibility for that limited position that we are in this world. Finiteness is the position of a creature, and we are creatures.

TWO: I would like to know if anyone has had the experience I have had. I am a TWO, and I went so far in my sickness that I became very ill, physically and mentally. I just gave and gave and gave until there was nothing more. I couldn't even breathe. Since that time — it's been four or five years now that I've been in recovery — I found it really difficult to want to give. I'm at a place now where it's almost like I'm pushing away my TWOness.

Richard: Let me speak to that. We're seeing this almost complete reversal in a lot of classic co-dependent types who are going into Twelve Step programs.

For a few years, their pendulum swings to the other extreme and their language becomes, "I've gotta meet my needs. I've got to meet my needs." After a while, their behavior seems almost sickening and you want to ask them, "Is there anything in your world other than your needs?"

But if we can just name that change of behavior as a necessary psychological pendulum swing, it would alleviate a lot of frustration. We could learn to trust you there for a while and let you play it out. After thirty years of meeting everybody else's needs, for a while you take care of yourself almost too much.

But you also know that that side of the pendulum is an extreme. I don't have to preach that to you.

You will find that mid-position again. You will reachieve an integration, an equanimity or homeostasis, which is the gift of the FOUR. This state reflects a harmony that realizes we can give out only to the degree we've learned how to take in. To reach this equanimity state, you've got to learn the new rules for taking in, and then you achieve that lovely contemplative balance of giving/receiving every day.

Giving and receiving is the balance all of us are searching for. You will realize that it is better to give *and* receive.

TWO: My fellow TWO, I certainly understand what you're saying. I'm currently in the process of a career shift. I think the difference between the "before" and the "now" in me is that now I'm being very selective.

I'm outlining what I want and what I don't want. I'm learning the art of saying no, thank God, and of saying yes to myself — here, which is very different for me. As I strategize this move, I am trying to be aware of it inside myself, not just out there.

But there's another side of me, the judging side, that says, "You're getting so lazy. You're not working as hard as you used to." I have to counter that by saying, "Thank God."

Richard: A lot of our first work — our first job or career — was compulsive. If we can really give people only who we really are, I think compulsive giving is seen by the other person as not really you. Our hand that feeds is not yet that "flesh for the life of the world."

And when I gave help to others out of my idealism and principles, maybe it was okay, but it wasn't something people could really chew on and really draw vitality and life from. We recognize one another's compulsive energy, and it does not truly satisfy.

It's the difference between falling in love when you're a twenty-year-old and falling in love when you're a mature person who knows how to love. The mature love feeds you. You say, "This I can rely upon. This is real. This is flesh for the life of the world" — instead of love that's not tested yet. Trouble is, we get married to one another at twenty.

Floor (Marge): I think that I went to the other side too. For most of my life, I gave a lot. I felt like a TWO. I think I went from the extreme of co-dependency to a preoccupation with taking care of myself. But the thing that is so wonderful about this workshop for me is the freedom of embracing myself and taking myself in my own arms — letting myself be who I am. There's a lot of joy and freedom in that, including the permission to play.

For years of my life I felt that I was on the wrong planet. I didn't express myself the way other people did. In recent years, however, I've noticed that my poetry has gotten to be more and more a part of me. I'm able to play more with people, and in my work I'm more creative and playful.

It seems that during this workshop we dwelled on the downside of our compulsion. We talked about that negative emphasis in our group last night. But there is also that part of us — the joy — that just wants to find expression. We don't always know how to let it happen.

FOUR: I feel drawn to oriental thought and philosophy and yet, at the same time, there's some sense that I should listen to people who seem to be journeying in the opposite direction from the way I feel and think.

My friends say, "Why are you going to listen to this person? You don't like that!" But for some reason I feel drawn to do it. Is this some need for balance that the FOUR has? My spiritual director happens to be a ONE, and I know that he gets me back off my tangents at times.

What Each Number Searches For

Richard: FOURs are usually described as searching for authenticity. ONEs are rather searching for balance. ONEs are obsessed with balance. With you, however, you are probably experiencing a balancing or integrating of different energies and sensitivities that is usually labeled as a "search for authenticity." It's much the same integration path we're all on.

Normally the integration path is a focus during the second half of life. We begin to see what we're not and what we've not experienced. If we're growing, if we're integrating, we naturally try to balance things in our lives.

According to Carl Jung, the need to achieve balance was true in every area of his typology except introvert-extrovert. I always like to point out that extroverts as they get older — I clearly saw this in myself as I turned forty — needed much more silence and solitude to know their center. We extroverts move to introversion. But the reverse is not true. The introverts do not become more extroverted. As Jung pointed out, the introvert becomes more introverted.

So what does that say?

The path of all humanity is moving toward introversion. When you see sixty-year-old people still wanting to run around Disneyland looking for more experience, such people — we'll make an exception for the SEVENs — are normally not growing.

And that is a challenge for the SEVEN. If you're growing, you desire to go inside. The phrase I always use is that the first half of life is text, the last half is commentary. After forty, you should be wanting to write your commentary. You need to go inside. If you stay outside too much after forty, you're not growing. I can make that statement as a universal. If you want to grow, you've got to have quiet time. This is why God made women fertile while they're young. So these children march through your life and out of it. Guess what happens when children keep coming back? How many parents have told me that they love their children, but want them to go away. [*Laughter*] "Go away; I need to live my own life."

I want to explain this to give you parents permission. You have every right to your solitude. That's what your soul is saying to you in the second half of life: "You need your solitude, you need your quiet; take it."

But that's a long commentary on what you said. We all need to balance ourselves. That's one of the healthiest things about the Enneagram — it gives us permission to balance ourselves. It encourages us not to stay on our compulsive track, but to trust the other side.

I hope that we all learn to trust the goodness in the other eight energies, all of which we have a little bit of.

Trusting the Inner Movements

FOUR: Richard, I've passed forty, obviously. As a FOUR, how do you handle looking inside as well as that sense of guilt that comes from thinking you've become too "I"-centered?

Richard: You know, that's a theme of mine, and I'm happy to talk on it. You want me to speak particularly to a FOUR?

Here's her scenario: she's a FOUR who has been drawn to go inside and also has that tremendous inner sensitivity that FOURs have; at present she's in the second half of life and she wants to make sure she doesn't get too involved in going inside so that she becomes too "I"-centered.

The quality you see in healthy FOURs is the potentiator. The FOUR moves toward empowering other people and making them special. That is, invariably, the FOUR movement, that fascination with specialness, with beauty, with fantasy. The healthy FOUR keeps asking, "How can I use that energy to empower other people?" Empowerers: that's what you are. As long as you keep empowering others and making them special, it will keep you from any extreme I-centeredness. Keep using that inner sensitivity, but keep using it to help make others special instead of sitting there in your throne of specialness.

You're right in your concern, however. If you go inside too much for too long, it becomes sick, maudlin, unhealthy depression. You've got to keep finding the specialness in the outer world and in other people.

Next, your task is to sift out from among those guilts what's healthy guilt and what's neurotic guilt. They are usually both mixed in there. Neurotic guilt has been handed on to us; it says, "Whenever we care for ourselves, that is selfishness." The question Christian religious folk often ask — "Is it from me or is it from God?" — is in some ways an unhealthy way to approach it. I hope the Ennea-gram gives you permission to ask, "Is it from me?" In itself, that's an okay question to start with. But then the next question for dis-cernment is, "If it is from me, what of it is leading toward life, integration, and vitality, and what of it is simply burrowing a hole inside the self?"

Don't be afraid to ask the question. I know we were trained that other way: "Is this from God or is this from me?" But if creation is already redemption, you can trust the inner movement when it is from you. How else would God speak to you; except through you? You're the listening station. God has to send the communication there.

By always doubting your own inner movements — "Oh, maybe it's not from God?" — and then looking elsewhere for God's grace, someplace really transcendent, we got into a phony religion. It's also phony transcendence.

You'll see a lot of religious people trying to pump up transcendent emotions by singing songs. There's nothing wrong with singing, but it's often used as part of a refusal to take the incarnational way.

God chose the enfleshed way, the creation of who we are. Listen to that message. If you begin to see yourself as the receiver station, you ask, "Okay, God, what are you saying here? What are you saying through my creation?" Now you are ready to ask the second ques-tion: "Which of this can be trusted unto life and which is going to lead me unto death?"

Both voices are there in you.

Don't trust any religion that pulls you too much into pseudo-transcendence. That's merely continuing the division between the secular and the sacred.

An important symbol at the death of Jesus is the tearing of the temple veil from top to bottom. What that symbolizes — the gospels are highly symbolic, theological documents — is that there is no division between the sacred and the secular anymore. That's why Jesus, as much as he loved and respected the Jewish temple as a good Jewish boy, said "It's gotta go. Because what that temple is doing is compartmentalizing the holy in one space in Jerusalem." That attitude tells us we've got to travel to Jerusalem to find the holy, and everything outside the temple is profane. When the tem-ple veil was torn from top to bottom at Jesus' death, that division was declared over and done with. In that symbol, Jesus was telling us, "You may no longer divide the world into the secular and the sacred."

After Christians have reflected upon Christ, even for two thousand years, we still continue to build our temples. And we tell ourselves that we have to go to the temples to find the holy. We observe this extinct rule, instead of listening to what Jesus is saying.

The body of Christ has taken the holy into the flesh, into the world. "I am the new temple," he says. The temple is now the body of Christ.

Who is the body of Christ?

Here it is. Us!

We still feel a little guilty at believing that. We say, "My God, this is bringing the divine down into the human." That's still a terrible scandal to us: that this group of people here is the living body of Christ. We are part of the seamless garment of the universal trust of life. As Thomas Merton says at one point, "If we really saw this, we would want to kneel before one another."

Now there's a man who has put it all together. If I really saw that this is the body of Christ, I would have to respect all life and reverence all life. I wouldn't have to run to a church to do that. It's here "among." That is the great, great turnaround; it is the turnaround that most religion never leads us to. Most religion keeps God up in his heaven and tells us that all is right with the world.

A Question of Balance

NINE: This comment has to do with balance. I'm a NINE. I was sitting here and I had an image of that V8 commercial where it shows a person leaning over on his side before he has his V8. I realized that as a NINE I have been completely overbalanced on the side of ONE, TWO, and THREE. Any one of those positions would make me feel comfortable in terms of feeling that I was good.

One of the things that a NINE has is a sense that right down at bottom there is really something inadequate. As I watched the panels, I really loved seeing the EIGHTs and the SEVENs. When I came here from Minnesota two days ago, I really had no sense of EIGHTs or SEVENs or SIXes. It was as though that side was just kind of blank. It was a real pleasure to see the EIGHTs and SEVENs, and I'm sorry I didn't go to dinner with some EIGHTs and SEVENs. [Laughter] I'd like to get some more of that energy; it was very helpful in balancing me.

Richard: NINEs often have to be encouraged to trust their EIGHT wing. EIGHTs possess the passion you need at times to get you out of your doldrums or your paralysis. That EIGHT wing is a good part of yourself, a part you want to go with and trust. Often the Enneagram gives NINEs permission to trust that EIGHT wing.

SIX: I have a question, Richard. You keep saying to "trust your wing." I'm a SIX with a very strong FIVE wing. Should I begin to develop my SEVEN wing?

Richard: That's a good idea. That's what we're talking about; it's your second-half-of-life stuff. Some people actually do start playing with both of their wings. Those will probably be people who move toward integration rather quickly.

Most of us develop one or another wing strongly in the first half of life, then experience a strong desire for the other in the second half. I know this primarily from experience. I can't document it from a study; I'm just sharing with you what I see.

But you're right at this point in your life to trust your SEVEN wing a lot more. I can't tell you how important it is for a SIX to lighten up! To go have some fun, to blow the rules once in a while. It's especially good for you to develop your SEVEN wing.

FOUR: Richard, you spoke about a FOUR needing to go to a FIVE, but as you look at the Enneagram diagram, there is such a breadth between those two numbers. Can you touch on that more fully?

Richard: That big space is deliberate and intentional because it is apparently a hard bridge to build. I'm not familiar personally with that space, but apparently it is a hard gap to overcome because it is between head and heart. Yet when it is accomplished, magic happens. There's a special power to it.

I don't know how to tell people to do it. Maybe some FOURs or FIVEs here could speak to the difficulty of it and what's helped you. It involves an aesthetic FOUR doing some more intellectual, foundational, objective FIVE work; or an intellectual FIVE reader trusting the more symbolic aesthetic heart space of the FOUR. Would any FOUR or FIVE want to speak to that?

FOUR: I'm a FOUR with a very strong FIVE wing. I have always been a reader from the time I was young, but if given the choice of being with people or reading a book I will choose to be with people. I think a FIVE would choose to be with the book. I'm a librarian also. Not a real public librarian, but a librarian at the church. I invented my own cataloging system: different! [*Laughter*] No Dewey decimal.

Reading is what I will do when I get stressed. I'll retreat into the quiet. I have to have quiet. I have to be able to read, and I love to have my books around. I may go out to a bookstore and spend a small fortune. I'll buy all these books and it may be years before I get around to reading them. But they're there and I like to have them nearby. I retreat into that. I find it easy to make that transition, whereas going to my THREE wing is hard.

FOUR: I'm a FOUR with a strong FIVE point. I grew up in rough circumstances in which I buried my FOUR and used my FIVE. My intellect and IQ took me a long way in the world. As I mature, I find I want to flirt a little bit with my THREE, have a little more fun, and lighten up. Just a bit, because I think the combination of FOUR and FIVE can be and feel a little heavy.

Richard: Thank you. Let's take a break.

17

The Enneagram's Spiritual Purpose

I would like to set the Enneagram in the context of its spiritual purpose. What is it really for? How can it help us bring life to the world? What can we do with it to develop ourselves and our families?

I'd like to begin with a quote from Aristotle, the great Greek philosopher whose ideas have been the basis of much Western thought. He said, "Freedom works only in a culture already committed to virtue; it cannot work otherwise."

Our culture seems to be a grand celebration of what people would like to call "freedom." But I don't think our culture, by and large, is any longer committed to virtue. It's committed mostly to the private self or the private group. Thus, we have groups vying against each other for their own freedoms and rights. It's this group against that group. People are into women's rights, gay rights, the rights of the poor, etc. They're all important rights, of course, but if each self-focused group is merely protecting its rights against the other, without anyone keeping the big picture in mind, we're not going to get anywhere as a society.

Inside such a society, the church cannot have much power because it is simply seen as one more group fighting for its own rights. Even within the church, there are groups fighting against other groups. It is seen, let's say, as conservatives vying with liberals for the freedom of religious groups instead of seeking the truth of religion, the truth of the soul, the truth of the spirit. I find, for example, that liberals are desperately in that position now. Certainly, they show no focus or clarity in defining what virtue is.

The question no one seems to be asking is: What is the truth beyond every person or group protecting their individual truth and their individual rights?

I want to pose that question to the Enneagram.

Trust in Our Divine Origins

I hope your understanding of the Enneagram doesn't lead you to overaggrandize or overglorify your own self. In many healthy ways, the Enneagram clearly puts us in the position of finite creatures. All of us ONEs in the world, for example, are at best but one-ninth of the truth. If you understand the Enneagram, it does not make you judgmental.

I can understand that when you first learn the Enneagram, you are eager to use the nine numbers to categorize yourself and others. As you begin to understand how this spiritual tool works, you may get involved for a while trying to explain everything and everybody by these numbers. But the Enneagram's objective is not to put people in a box; it's to take them out of a box, until there finally is no box.

We're each a creature that reflects a part of the divine image. Each of us has a divine origin, a divine origin we can trust. That's the difference. Instead of focusing on hatred, denial, doubt, or running away, our focus should be on trust in our divine origins.

Our main problem is we doubt our divine origin. We avoid the abyss of God's otherness and God's beyondness because that's too much to comprehend. Instead, what I slip into — and almost drown in — is the variety and mystery of all the other types, all those different energies where I'm not at home and which I don't understand. If you do not know yourself, your true self "hidden with Christ in God" (Col. 3:3), you will invariably live out of other people's *image* of you or your own *image* or yourself — neither of which are substantial truth.

So I, and most of us, try to pull everybody into our type and judge everybody else as bad because they're not a ONE. "Why aren't you a ONE? Why aren't you a good boy? Why don't you follow the rules and do what I feel I have to do?"

There's a certain kind of resentment that's in us ONEs. I don't know if it's in you. "Dammit," we say, "I worked so hard, while you enjoy yourself. Why are you enjoying yourself, you SEVENs? I never let myself enjoy myself." In ONEs, there's a certain resentment that you haven't done it my way.

You all have your own kind of resentment — each of you in your own way. For example, you FIVEs look upon the rest of us as so uneducated, so plebeian and unthinking, out there dealing with messy feelings instead of substantial objective truth, which you presume you have. [*Laughter*]

The contemplative journey involves going back to your divine origin. The journey is not concerned primarily with thinking, feeling, or gut responses, even though we all get trapped in one or other of those three centers. The journey is about going back to pure being, the foundation underneath it all, who we are in God.

Spirituality, therefore, is always about love, the foundation of reality. All of the great world religions are saying the same thing:

underneath it all is this great mystery called love. We cannot manage or organize ourselves into love. It is a source that is revealed to us and uncovered for us. We break through to it, or better, it breaks through to us. All we can do is get ourselves out of the way and let it reveal itself. The events of reality, our relationships, and the paths we're on are all merely windows and doors to the love that is the foundation of all things. This Love is something, or better, Someone who can be trusted. Love says that I am standing on holy ground, that it is a benevolent and finally safe universe, that God is on my side.

Trust in Reality

I have a bone to pick with religion when it tells us that reality is not trustworthy. To assert this is, in effect, to say there is no God. That's atheism posing as religion. Many religious people are in that sense atheistic, because they put no real trust in pure being.

Intuitively, each of us knows that the foundation is trustworthy and can be moved with. To the FOURs, the world seems so tawdry and disappointing that they go inside to find the mystery; inside it is beautiful and they want to stay there, but they also want to bring it back out and share it. We ONEs find the trustworthy mystery through the law and principles; we discover a set of principles to give order back to the world. The FIVEs go into their minds and try to find the mystery in holy ideas. The THREEs try to find their trust in a world that works, that fits together, so they can organize and manage it.

All of us are striving to break through the shadow and disguise all around us and in us, because we cannot live in a world of absurdity. If the world is meaningless — if it came from nowhere and it's going nowhere — then life is meaningless. I think that's why fundamentalists often have such resistance to evolutionary theory, because they think that creation cannot be evolutionary and that evolution cannot reflect God's creation. For me there is no conflict. It's the same reality. But they are afraid that evolution is saying that creation is meaningless.

Both sides agree that the soul cannot deal with meaninglessness.

In *Man's Search for Meaning*, Viktor Frankl said that what finally killed people in the death camps was the fear and the anxiety that, after all was said and done, life didn't mean anything. People will go crazy if they have to believe that it's all meaningless, that God's creation is all "sound and fury signifying nothing," that we came into this world for no purpose and we're leaving for no purpose.

Religion, in its healthiest sense, tells you that life means something. It tells you that you came from somewhere, specifically that you were created by God. In the *Baltimore Catechism*, the answer to the first question — Who made you? — is "God made you." That answer may sound simple and obvious to you, but there are a lot of people who don't believe it anymore. They believe only in the self, without accepting any philosophical underpinnings for that belief.

One implication of that self-focused belief is you now have to find inside yourself your "raison d'être," the explanation for your own existence. That is too much of a burden for any human. To attempt it, you would have to be inflated; you would have to make yourself a lot more important than you are and take yourself too seriously.

Nevertheless, even if you've taken that road, hopefully it will lead you through to humor, light-heartedness, surrender, and letting go of yourself.

As authentic religious people, we do not have to take ourselves too seriously: "You're just a creature among billions who happened to come around in this one little century, in this one little moment of time, and you're going to be gone in a few years. At best, you're an expression of one-ninth of the truth — or one-nine-hundredth or one nine-thousandth of the truth."

To realize that is freedom. Healthy religion is also freedom. Too many of us have been fed a strong dose of unhealthy religion. When I see most of the country acting against that unhealthy side of religion, I can understand why.

A People on a Journey

But self-aggrandizement is not what we were given in the great Judaeo-Christian tradition. To those of you who are Jewish, I would like to affirm that Christianity makes no sense without its Jewish roots and its very personal Jewish God. Unless people understand healthy Judaism, they don't have a chance of understanding healthy Christianity.

Many of those who are indoctrinated in pseudo-Christianity are not grounded in that marvelous sense of this personal God by whom the Jewish people were led out of slavery and into freedom. God was their liberator. The Jewish journey always starts with God as liberator. The pattern is that they are enslaved people and God leads them from slavery to freedom.

How angry I sometimes get (it's a necessary righteous anger of a ONE!) that we've turned religion around and let it lead people back into slavery. In true religion, Yahweh, the God of Israel, is always leading the people into a great and spacious place (Exod. 3:8).

The first reference to salvation occurs in the book of Exodus. As the Jewish people were beginning to hear this faint and wonderful voice of God, it led them on a collective journey. The promise of salvation they heard was that God was leading them to a "land rich and broad," which became Israel.

Almost everyone is fascinated by this country of Israel, positively and negatively. One reason is because in our Scriptures Israel became the symbol of the great and spacious land of the soul.

The great and spacious land that is given on the spiritual journey is not the geography of Israel but the spacious place inside the soul where there's room for *everything*, all parts of the truth.

The Enneagram is a way to look at the face of God without it being merely a reflection of my own face.

Ideally, in religion, we radically discover who we are. That's the contemplative journey — going back to the center where we discover the answer to the question: "Who am I in God?" The contemplative path is not focused on believing in all kinds of dogmas and theories, but on believing that I came forth from God and I will return to God. In contemplation, you learn to believe that this movement can be trusted, that underneath it all is Love, and that Love is a Person.

The saints are quite aware that Love is not something they strive for or work up to or "take courses" on. For the saints, life is the great love course. When Love breaks through into your life, you know the truth of it. Maybe it happens looking at a sunset — that's the classic image. Maybe it happens looking at your beloved. Maybe it comes in a moment of insight — as it might for a FIVE. Maybe it's a gut intuition of the foundational justice and truth of all things that an EIGHT would recognize.

Whenever you discover Love, you want to thank somebody for it. You know you didn't create it. You know you are not the Love; you're just participating in it. Vincent dePaul understood this; he would thank poor people for letting him help them. "Thank you for letting me love you, for you open the window that lets me see Love."

You do come to that moment where you recognize that Love is the foundation. You realize that Love shows itself every so often, that we are merely searchers and discoverers. We do not create the pattern. It is already there.

Legitimate Pain

If we do not face the "legitimate pain" of letting-go-into-Love, we will eventually be faced with a pain ten times more demanding because we have lived our illusions and avoided *what-is*, the foundational Love. Religion often covers up Love. Even worse, it tells us that we can find it only by correct behavior; this is the lie that the

ONE often believes. "I will get Love if I do everything right." The basic problem for us ONEs is worthiness. For us, everything is keeping a ledger, keeping accounts. We look at our ledger and ask: "Have we deserved this much? Have we worked to deserve this much joy? Okay, then I'll let myself receive it." The ONE is constantly keeping a ledger, constantly noting assets and debits.

"Have I been a good enough boy to have this much ecstasy now?" If I haven't, I will actually self-deaden and self-deny and not let myself enjoy the ecstasy. I know the Enneagram and I teach it, yet I can't stop keeping my ledger. That's how trapped I am, how ONEish I am.

It's hard to believe that the compulsions in all of us could be that deep.

Jung says, "If you get rid of the pain before you have answered its question, you get rid of the Self along with it."

Pain always brings with it some questions that must be answered. Now, this talk about facing pain isn't just a sermon to SEVENs; it's to all of us. The pain comes to all of us; if you get rid of it too quickly, without learning its lesson, you get rid of the Self along with it.

That "Self" word is often capitalized by Jung. As far as I can see, Jung used Self as the closest word, in many ways, for God. Our Christian term for Self is "the body of Christ." In my mind, it's just different terminology. The body of Christ is the big Self that includes all us little selves.

Jung's observation is also true of the little self. If you dismiss the pain before you have answered its question, you not only get rid of the big Self, the experience of God, but you also get rid of your own self. Our Christian metaphor for that pain is the cross.

Answering *the question* of the pain and the darkness is the way through it. It involves facing your compulsion and facing the lie — the false image — that each of us has of God.

Part of the reason our compulsion hangs on so tenaciously and for so long is that we are all desperately attached to a certain self-image. It takes humility to admit this attachment, and even such humility must be asked for!

Surrendering Self-Images

For some dumb reason, I need to think of myself as a "good boy." That self-image has given me security and identity; it got me through the first thirty-five years of my life. I've played the "good boy" game so long, it's carved a neural groove in my brain. And I don't know how to get out of that neural groove.

On the one hand, that self-image has been very helpful to me. It's the way I learned to pay attention to reality. It's the way I got my energy. It motivated me through the seminary, the priesthood, the Community of New Jerusalem, and now into the Center for Action and Contemplation. It worked quite well in a lot of situations. It gave me a way to be and act in the world successfully. It drove me. My genius is anger. I'm good at it. I'm good at being focused and clear. I know what I have to do and what price I'll pay for it. So why change that self-image now?

(By the way, forgive me for not doing this analysis with each one of you, but I'm sure you can transfer what I'm explaining about myself to your own compulsions.)

Just as I did, each of you found a way and it's worked for you. Your own neural groove has carried you successfully through most of your life.

But I want you at this point to face the part of you that is *attached* to that image.

What the contemplative journey is about, what all the great mystics talk about, is a journey that surrenders self-image. That's why Franciscans use the language of poverty (other traditions use words like "emptiness," "nothingness," "no-mind," "abandonment," etc.). They realize that their true richness and glory may be found not in themselves but in their divine origin, in the divine center that is God. It means I don't need to have any private self to protect anymore. Paradoxically, poverty in that sense is total riches because when I let go of the false self, I am everything.

No one expresses it better than St. Francis when he says in effect, "I don't need to protect anything; therefore I've got everything."

Nothing is mine; therefore everything is mine. I don't need to possess anything. The trees are mine, the heavens are mine, the earth is mine, the animals are mine. It's all mine.

We paid a high price to protect our individualism, our ego boundaries, our false self-image. We asked our self-image: "Do you like it? Does it look good? Does it meet your needs?" We even offered incense to it.

The price we paid for self-image was giving up spiritual riches and spiritual freedom.

The spiritual journey is always about the surrender of our attachment to our self-image, the letting go of self-image. I invite us all to look at our own self-image.

TWOs, for example, should reflect on the ways they want to look like a helper or their belief that everyone will like them if only they act like Goody-Two-Shoes and wash the other guy's feet. Do you see how living out a helper self-image is solving *your* problem, not necessarily ours. See if you can feel an attachment to your self-image as a helpful person.

Then just blow it away! I give you all permission to blow your self-image. You don't need to look like what you think you need to look like. Let go of those ego boundaries that protect, advertise, and promote the self in each case.

That's why we ONEs usually do a little bad thing on the side now and then. First, we do it in secret so no one else knows, and we take a secret satisfaction in being bad boys. But as long as no one else knows about it, we don't have to give up our self-image.

What we've got to do is blow the image publicly. I did that when I first said "shit" on a published cassette! [*Gales of laughter*] To the outspoken EIGHTs that must seem like, "Wow, big deal!" [*More gales of laughter*] But for me to use that word in polite society was really daring, and I actually did lose some friends over it. People here in this city got all upset! "He uses bad words." "He's not a good priest."

And then all the guilt comes, as you ONEs know. "See, see, what they say is true." Do you know why some people get upset? They want to keep you in your compulsion. They like you there. Your family and your friends especially have gotten used to you there. As far as they are concerned, you're not allowed to blow it.

Thus, we need you SEVENs to be the clowns, so don't you dare come and be serious and talk in the corner about something that matters. We want you to play the clown; we want you in your box.

What we call the "real world" is precisely what boxes us in and affirms the false self. True spirituality calls forth the true self.

Faith to Let Go

With the Enneagram, we're not trying to put one another into a box or to stay in one ourselves. We're trying to get out of our boxes.

Again I emphasize: becoming un-boxed is a spiritual task. It will not happen by ego-consciousness or too much ego-focus, which is often the most that a purely psychological approach can offer you.

With its many self-help books, psychology offers you techniques and methods, words and jargon. There is nothing wrong with self-help books. They are often about effectiveness and control. They respond to your question, "How can I control and change myself?"

That's not what spirituality is about. Spirituality is about surrender, not control. It's about letting go, handing it over, realizing someone else has to do it.

I'm talking traditional stuff here. This is the world of prayer: "God, you have to do it to me. I don't know how to do it. I don't know how to make it happen because the only way I make things happen is in a ONE way. If I attack my ONE self-image, I only exercise and strengthen my ONE energy. I'll only be using my same ONE zeal, focus, and dedication to stop trying to be a ONE!"

Therefore, I've got to live the humiliated life, walking around knowing you people are seeing me as a ONE. "He's in it again."

I'm sure the staff recognizes me when I'm in it. "Richard's into his ONE again." They probably just look the other way.

At this point, I've got to be humble enough to say, "Yup, I know. That's the little person I am. I cannot *not* be this ONE. I hope you can accept me as being one-ninth of the truth."

But you're also one-ninth of the truth. That's the great mercy that allows us to accept and free one another.

Faith, for me, means letting go of the images, until you feel like nothing. *Nada. Nihil.* That's why faith is so rare. Religion is rather common, but faith is rather rare, because no one wants to live between first and second base, in that in-between space where you're not sure you're going to make it to second base.

"I'd prefer to stay securely on first base and be a neurotic ONE rather than live in the space where I let go of my ONEness and yet am not sure I'm going to make it all the way to second base."

Faith happens in the interstices, during the interruptions and on the thresholds. Faith happens only when I leave this room where I feel in control. In this room I maintain my self-explanation, my ego boundaries, a moral sense of my own rightness and my moral superiority. We all have rooms like that — not just ONEs.

We're all looking for the moral high ground. Maybe your search is not as moralistic as a ONE does it, but we all do it to try to feel right. It's called self-salvation. We try to pull ourselves up by our own bootstraps and say, "I'm okay."

In contrast, justification by faith means I stop trying to pull myself up by my own bootstraps, stop any process of self-justification or self-validation.

Do you realize the kind of surrender we're talking about? It's very rare because it cuts to the root of our ego-centrism.

Only God can lead you on that path.

Normally it will happen in spite of yourself. It usually happens through humiliation (forgive me, SEVENs), failure (sorry, THREEs), not being right (too bad, ONEs), suffering, grief, and loss.

Unless you listen to the questions the pain offers, you will not go through the pain to life and the true self. We've got to listen to the questions that pain, suffering, humiliation, and rejection offer us when the game doesn't work.

Hopefully that happens by the middle of life. Everyone can usually get through the pain. Besides, God often gives us some grace period. As we know, many little kids who have to suffer grow up real quick, as long as they ask themselves the questions that pain offers.

Here again is the paschal mystery. Half of life is death; half of life is ecstasy.

FOURs, don't go so much into the maudlin pain of things that you are afraid of the ecstasy. SEVENs, don't go too much into the ecstasy that you avoid the pain. All the rest of us are somewhere in between. Both ecstasy and pain have their truth to teach us. That is why I believe Jesus is not really telling us to "be good"; he simply tells us to "follow him" through passion, death, and resurrection.

For now, our purpose is to recognize the trap of self-image and to learn how not to be attached to it. It will still be there, but don't advertise it, don't protect it, don't move with it too much. Don't be too "good" because it will only be according to your definition of goodness anyway. "God alone is good" (Mark 10:18).

Every faith crisis seems to start when the old images don't work anymore. If you're growing, you should have a major or minor faith crisis every three to five years.

The Struggles of Faith

People who don't mature religiously are people who stay on first base. They hang on tightly to their infantile, even dysfunctional, image of God, even when they picture God as a terrorist who undercuts and deadens them. In effect, they say, "That's the one God. I'm going to keep him, because he's the only God I know. I'm going to keep him, even though we're killing one another here on first base. I'm the righteous little boy and he's the judgmental little God. We've got a nice little dysfunctional relationship going here on first base."

This describes most of civil religion, cultural Christianity as I see it, and cultural Judaism too. We stay here fighting it out and killing one another, God killing us and us killing God, pretending we love God when it's obvious to everybody else that we don't.

Helen Keller was a woman who was blind and couldn't hear; yet she attained enormous wisdom. Toward the end of her life, she wrote, "Sometimes I fear that religion is, in fact, man's despair at *not* finding God."

We practice our religious rituals to placate this angry, distant God. We just keep offering the incense and going to the services, reading the Bible and getting self-justification, precisely because we haven't experienced that radical other-justification: that I am hidden with Christ in God, that I came forth from God and I will return to God, and in between I learn how to dance.

That's all. I have to learn how to dance. It's obvious God doesn't demand that we dance perfectly, just that we dance: that we stay in the process, stay on the journey, stay on the path all the way through.

During every faith crisis, one or other of our images falls apart. It's either the self-image that we hold on to feverishly, or the God image that we hang on to tightly. That's the unfortunate conservatism of religion. It says, "Don't question my God image. If you do, it means you're a disbeliever." And further, let's use this toxic image of God as a validation for a static and often sick image of myself. What we lose out on is what we were created for: Love.

People who really believe are people who know how to doubt. Healthy doubt is the other half of faith, and if you tell me you don't know how to doubt, I don't believe your faith. What you have is religion, not faith.

Real faith struggles, like Jacob and the angel, wrestling with the mystery of God. "Who are you?" Jacob asked the angel. "Where did you come from? What are you asking of me? I know who you are, but what is your name?" (Gen. 32:38).

The Jewish people were wise. They wouldn't give a name to God. They understood the first commandment. There was to be no name for God, because when you give a name to God, you think you understand God and you stop the journey. You stay on first base — or whatever base you happen to be on at the time.

Instead of respecting the fact that we really can have no name for God, we've gone far too quickly into creating our icons, our metaphors, our images of God to help us name God. But instead of worshiping God, we worship these metaphors and icons. We sit safely on first base instead of continuing forward on the journey to the nameless God.

In Latin, the divinity was called *Deus absconditus*, the hidden, always-hiding God. God remains in hiding not for the sake of non-relationship, but to pull us, tease us, seduce us more and more deeply into the mystery of relationship by remaining always a bit hidden and a bit beyond.

If we are to move and grow spiritually, there must be a periodic surrender of our self-image and of our self-serving God image.

Unfortunately, religion uses most of its energy to maintain self-image and God image. When religion doesn't help you let go of images, it is not true religion — I don't care what denomination or sect it is. One's as bad as the other at the immature levels. Each of them have you worshiping the means instead of the end; they would have you adore the path instead of walking the journey to the end. Arguing about the message to avoid the Messenger.

Listening to God Everywhere

We protect our methods, means, and formulas. We prefer nurturing our doctrines and our denominational forms instead of facing the really terrifying contemplative journey into nothingness. Leaping into the darkness of surrender is what faith means to me. "Faith" is simply our theological word for that humble, uncertain, but choiceful response to every new revelation. In faith, we wait for new revelation.

Faith and revelation are correlative terms. You don't have new faith unless you have new revelation. And revelation cannot happen unless there is a believer there to receive it. Faith and revelation are like a lover and a beloved. There's a handing back and forth. Revelation goes deeper into the mystery only when faith is there to receive it.

Our Catholic tradition, I'm proud to say, has never been afraid of the mind. We never believed that revelation came only from the Bible. Never. This has been the source of some contention between us and some forms of Protestantism.

In Catholic theology, revelation began about fifteen billion years ago with the first act of creation. God didn't wait until the last second — when the Bible arrived on the planet — to reveal who God is.

If you put the entire creation of this planet on a hypothetical year's timeline, with Divine creation beginning at the stroke of midnight January 1 and today being December 31, homo sapiens appears the last three minutes of December 31. That means the whole Judaeo-Christian tradition occurs in the last second of December 31.

Do you really think God waited until the last second to tell us who God is? Absurd. Revelation didn't begin with the Bible. That belief, I think, is the Achilles heel of some forms of Protestantism that believe it is only the Bible we should listen to.

No, we listen to experience, we listen to our soul, our mind, and the world. We look at all of it and say, "These are the footprints and fingerprints of God."

For those who need the Bible to establish this position, you'll find it in Romans 1:20. God is known in the revelation of things as they are. It's right there in the Bible — if you need it to be there.

Our task on the spiritual journey is to look at things as they are in all their stages, in their agony and in their ecstasy. Life, everywhere, will be your best teacher. That's why I'm ashamed of Catholics who are fighting the Enneagram (and it's mostly coming from Catholics at this point). They don't know their own tradition.

Our tradition has always known how to integrate everything that was real and true. For example, I quoted Aristotle at the beginning of this chapter. Thomas Aquinas interpreted "pagan" Aristotle and integrated his classical Greek thought with Catholicism in his *Summa Theologica*. At first, Aquinas was called a heretic for doing this, but later his *Summa* became the primary textbook in priestly seminary training and remained so for four hundred years.

Integration has always been our tradition. Pull it in. See if it fits. If it truly can't be integrated, it isn't Christ. Orthodoxy and heresy are necessary and important categories; it's just that they often seem to change places!

Christ is the whole One who includes and integrates all things. If God is truth, we have no truth to fear. Whether it be psychological, political, metaphysical, scientific, or evolutionary truth—if it's truth, it's of God. We don't need to be afraid of it. The important question is not "Where did it come from?" The important question is "Is it true?" "If it is true, it is from the Holy Spirit" (St. Thomas Aquinas).

How else are we going to achieve any integrity or wholeness except through that kind of approach? That's Catholicism at its best.

But I find there are so few Catholics today who want to include all things in Christ—that's the meaning of the word "catholic." "According to the whole" (*kata holon*) is what the word says in Greek. To be Catholic is to try to pull it all together.

I'm afraid we've had a lot more provincialism than catholicism. We've had a lot more ethnicity than catholicity. Catholicism must include our Hebrew and Islamic roots. True Catholicism just keeps moving out and including whatever it meets: there's always room for the other. There's room for it all in the Cosmic Christ. Christ is not fragile, tiny, and in need of our protection.

Always toward a Bigger God

We students of the Enneagram reply, "I don't know if I'm ready for a Christ that big." As J. B. Phillips used to say to his students, "Your God is too small."

We want to hold on to our small God, while faith is always leading us to a bigger God and to a bigger world, which must include all the genders, all the races and religions, and, finally, all that God is doing — and God is doing everything. That's what we believe. God is in all things, giving energy to all things; therefore I must respect all things. I must be willing to see God in all things: people of other races and religions, experiences and cultures. The divine image is in *all* that God has created.

Do you know how many surrenders that involves? How many acts of faith that is?

Jesus took faith to the end point, the climactic point. In the Sermon on the Mount, he's building up to it — the church hasn't arrived there yet. He puts it all in the simple formula: "You must love your enemies." He carries love to the farthest degree of otherness: those who hate you, mistreat you, and do ill to you. If you don't love them, Jesus says, you're not into the great mystery yet.

You haven't broken through the shadow and the disguise until you can actually find a way within yourself to love even those who hurt you. That state is nothing you can self-generate. You can't talk yourself into loving people who have made your life hard. And somehow the grace is given. You ask and wait for it. It is a surrender, an uncovering, a discovery, a gift, a revelation — it's there.

You wait for it, though, and you wait in hope, as Simone Weil says. You wait in hope and you keep asking.

What's happening on this journey is that the soul is being carved out and opened up so there is room for this grace. That's all.

You're being changed.

God isn't saying, "Well, I might not want to give the grace to that person." God isn't refusing grace; it's just that you're not ready to receive it. When the student is ready, the teacher arrives.

The spacious land, the New Israel, has to be carved out in your soul so you can live in the Promised Land. Joshua goes in and opens up the land. That's the job of life: to go in and open up the land.

Again, *you* don't do it; it is done to you. You don't change yourself; you are changed. For the most part we are changed in spite of ourselves. All we can do is get ourselves out of the way and invite the grace.

A Gift of Freedom

The Enneagram I offer you is a tool. It is not necessary for salvation. If you've done your inner work, you've recognized by the time you're forty that you're too much this or that. You're an overstatement in one direction. You're too much of one thing. You can see that you're not fully alive, that you're always drawing your energy from one source, that you're almost always focused on one kind of reality, that you have your peculiar way of solving problems. And you can also see that your little self is not the Real, it is not the big Self, it is not the big Truth.

The Enneagram is offering you the gift of freedom. I think the reason why a lot of people are going to continue to be afraid of the Enneagram is because it offers too much freedom.

When I start telling you that you can trust yourself, imagine someone who was never told, "You can trust yourself." You don't have to look very far to find people who don't trust themselves. Almost every religious voice we've ever heard said things like, "Don't trust yourself. Don't trust your experience. Don't look at your heart. Don't trust your feelings. Don't trust your reason and your mind."

And here I am telling you that you can trust all of them. You can trust your gut, your heart, and your head. For most people, that's too much freedom. So I expect the Enneagram will continue to be criticized by many people.

Freedom works only in a culture committed to virtue. We can't expect this country to be culturally committed to virtue. That, ideally, was supposed to be the mystery of the church. And we may not even have a church that is committed to virtue.

St. Augustine put it clearly: "Love God and do whatever you want."

SIXes get so afraid when they hear statements like "Love God and do whatever you want." They say, "No, No, No!" But SIXes must remember that God is working together with you (Rom. 8:28) to bring about good in all things — even your sin. "For those who love God, all things will work together for the good."

Just stay on the path, the path toward love. It's the only path. What God's trying to do is bring us *by our free choice into the love God is.*

Each decision, each moment, each faith crisis is a chance for another "yes." God is expanding your freedom so your yesses can be more free. Usually pain is the only way to do that. When you don't feel like saying the yes, you go down deep.

I had some darkness about a month ago and I felt it was drawn out of me by grace in a wonderful way. I don't know where the darkness came from or where it went. But I know that in that darkness I had to dig to a place that I didn't know I had — and find a yes.

When you can trust, as Gerald May says, that there's a part of you that has always said yes to God, then you can trust your soul. God is within you. Even though you've journeyed down a lot of dead-ends and made some mistakes, even those dead-ends will be turned completely around by God, if it's necessary — that's the providence of God.

Trust that even your dead-ends, your mistakes, even your sins were ultimately misguided attempts at love. Be honest with yourself: even your sexual forays, even your drugs, even your alcoholism were misguided attempts to find the great love. Your heart of hearts said, "I know that the foundation of reality is Love."

We know that. It's written in our souls because we came forth from Love. It's what we can't forget. True religion reminds us that we've all forgotten what our soul already knows. When we see God, it will not be a new discovery; it will be a recognition. It will be a profound recognition of that heart and soul of ourselves that is *al-*

ready in union with God. All contemplation and all true prayer are attempts to go back to that place of primary and primal union.

My hope in giving the Enneagram is that it will be an aid and a gift on that journey toward a Great Compassion — a compassion toward yourself and toward all the other eight types of sisters and brothers who are found on the Enneagram. The Great Compassion is not manufactured or even learned; it is first of all seen. God is not "held" as much as God is be-held.

18

Images of God

For the church, the presence of Christ is represented primarily in the assembly of the faithful. If you like, you can see our gathering community as the body of Christ coming together.

There are two other presences of Christ we speak of in liturgical worship: the Eucharist and the Scriptures. The Eucharist is Christ in material reality, and the Scriptures are Christ in the word. Both of these presences, however, are derived from the presence of Christ in the community.

The primary presence of Christ is in people, just as the primary presence of God is in God's creation. The scriptural word and the sacrament are merely attempts to focus that primary presence.

During the first thousand years in the church, the assembly of the faithful was spoken of as the *Corpus Verum*, the True Body. The people were perceived as the true body of Christ. The Eucharist was called the *Corpus Mysticum*, the Mystical Body of Christ. During the second thousand years, those two terms were completely turned around due to all kinds of historical circumstances, so that today the people are called the Mystical Body of Christ and the Eucharist is called the *Corpus Verum*, the True Body of Christ.

I think the first thousand-year tradition is closer to the reality. The gathering of those assembled to celebrate the Eucharist is the *Corpus Verum*, the True Body of Christ. The bread I hold in my hands at the Eucharist is the *Corpus Mysticum*, the Mystical Body of Christ.

The reason Catholicism has hung on to this representation of Christ-God in bread so strongly is that it connects the sacred and the secular. It's saying you can trust material reality. If we can trust that God is in something as mundane as bread and God is in something as dangerous as intoxicating wine, there you have the mystery.

Throughout the centuries, Catholics held on feverishly to this tenet of faith. The belief in Christ's presence in the bread and the wine is almost the touchstone of Catholic orthodoxy.

I know that may seem like an overstatement to some people, but if we lose that belief, we lose the union of the sacred and the secular, the coming back together of heaven and earth. I want you to see the

Eucharist as a representation and an integration of all that is, not just as a way to get holy. The Eucharist is a naming of what is holy, and it's saying that all things are holy, even bread and wine. Even dangerous things like intoxicating wine.

Jung makes a great deal of the symbol of wine. He says he finds it interesting that in so many languages, the word "spirit" is used for liquor. In the liturgy, we lift up the cup of wine as holy. Wine and other forms of alcohol have probably caused pain in some of your lives, yet we say, "This too is Christ."

Who Is God?

Sin and potential sin are also potential grace. And that place where you can be most wounded is also the place where you can be most gifted.

The Jewish tradition said the same thing with the holding up of the serpent in the desert. The people were bitten by the serpent, and Yahweh said, "Hold up the snake. The very thing that bit you will be the thing that saves you." The poison is itself the antidote (Num. 21:8–9).

According to the Enneagram, your sin is your gift. It's just a modern way of saying what we've always said, even in the Bible. The history of sin and the history of salvation are one and the same book.

We come before the loving God as people, compulsive, addictive, attached, driven, and trapped. We don't know how to untrap ourselves. We ask for God's mercy. We ask for God's grace to free us from our THREEness and FIVEness and EIGHTness.

One simple reading from Exodus points to what I have been explaining about the Enneagram: "I am Yahweh, your God, who brings you out of Egypt where you lived as slaves. You shall have no other gods except me" (Exod. 20:1–3).

God is bringing the people on their journey to focus and purity of heart. Purity of heart means "to will one thing, to stay on one path." That's a summation of what Jewish monotheism was seeking to do — to bring the people to a relationship with the one God who had created them, so their adorations were not wasted on what was not God.

This God said to them: "You shall not make for yourselves any images or likenesses of anything in heaven above or on the earth below. You shall not bow down before these images. You shall not serve them. For I, Yahweh, your God, am a jealous God."

"A jealous God" — isn't that an interesting phrase? You wouldn't think of God as jealous. Maybe the FOURs understand a jealous God. God wants all — everything — of us.

As we continue faithfully on the journey, we start experiencing that jealousy. We sense that there's someone out after me. There's a God "on the make," which the TWOs understand. This is a God who wants me to surrender all of me, and this God keeps waiting and pursuing me until my surrender is offered.

The first commandment is telling us not to be attached to any image of God. So not only do we have a self-image that we are attached to, but I think we all have a conflicting or even a false God image. And, for some reason, we are attached to it. We were commanded not to carve something that we could get into a dysfunctional relationship with, but rather to allow God to keep revealing Godself — until we have the "naked" person before the "naked" God, and we can make love. Allow God this freedom and God in turn will allow us freedom.

In contemporary society we have a strong example of our unwillingness to let God be free. Many people insist on a masculine image of God. Now, if you're not ready to let go of God as a purely masculine image, you're not going to be ready to go to second or third base where God is just as much woman as man. Whatever maleness means, whatever femaleness means, that's who God is in God's totality.

A lot of people are afraid of a female God. What does that say — especially when a *woman* is afraid of a female God? What does that say about her attitude toward her own body? Toward her own soul? I've found such women. They can be some of the angriest people, when I've dared to speak of God as feminine. Some women can get really upset. You'd love to know their mother relationship, wouldn't you? You'd love to know how they are connected to the important women in their lives. Or maybe there aren't any.

Nine False Images of God

"You shall not have strange gods before you" (Exod. 20:2). Let's go through, rather quickly, nine conflicting or destructive images of God, which might be fruit for future meditation.

The opposite of *symbiosis* (which means "life with") we could call *synthanatotic* (which means "death with"). The Enneagram suggests there is a synthanatotic relationship between our compulsion and our God image. Instead of living together, we die together if our God image is false or "strange."

The God Image of ONEs. The God of the ONEs is the God who keeps the ledger. For ONEs, God is a judge who is constantly analyzing whether I'm worthy and whether I did it right. He's the great

Pantocrator, the Great Christ who doesn't look like a human being at all. You see this image of God represented in the Cathedral of the Immaculate Conception in Washington, D.C.

This God image is majestic; he's a powerful male God. He's really God the Father who has all power within himself. Besides, he has this great eye that sees everything. Look at the eye that is on every dollar bill. That's the God of the ONE. He's watching me.

Bette Midler recorded a song — I don't know if I like it or dislike it — which has the line, "From a distance he's watching us." In the song, I think it's a benevolent God watching, but I'm not sure. For me, if God is watching from a distance, God is keeping a ledger.

That's the God that we ONEs somehow attached ourselves to. We still carry within us a terrible fear.

Despite all my theology and my hopeful prayer, that divine Judge is still the one who's up there, out there watching from a distance — and I'd better be a good boy.

This God of ONEs is basically a glorified Santa Claus. "I don't want to get coal for Christmas. I want to get presents."

Until we get into dialogue with that God and recognize that such a false "image" isn't talking back — until we recognize that our god is a "strange" god — we won't go any further. We'll stay on first base.

The God Image of TWOs The God of the TWOs is best represented in Catholic iconography as the Sacred Heart of Jesus. He holds his heart — this pumping, red heart — out in front. It is the image of God as one waiting to be seduced. If you're a TWO and this is your God image, you say to yourself, "I've got to romance this God. I've got to play out the game of love. I've got to bargain the chips of love with this God. I've got to play the love-game better than he does."

For the TWOs, God isn't doing his job of love very well. That reflects the pride of the TWO, who then says, "I've got to do it better. God's just not at all sufficiently loving the people in this hospital. God's not taking care of them. God's not nursing them. I'm going to be the great nurse and I will be the love of God."

TWOs are almost trying to seduce this God into their own perception of what love is. Which, of course, is a false love-perception and therefore it produces a destructive God-relationship.

God doesn't have to be romanced and seduced. God is already on your side. You are already beloved.

TWOs must surrender to the experience of already being beloved; they don't have to convince this God that they're loving and worthy of being loved. They will discover that they are falling in love with a God whose love is larger than their love. God, as John says, is always larger than your heart, always more than you expected (1 John 3:20).

TWOs, let your God be larger than your love. Don't get into a love-competition with God. Let God *need* you even more than you think you need love.

The God Image of THREEs. For the THREE, God is clearly the co-creator who isn't working fast enough. Did you ever see that drawing by William Blake of God as the divine architect using a compass on a cosmic design?

The THREE God is the divine architect, the co-creator God who's drawing up a master plan for the world, and I, the THREE, have to get in there and master plan with God. The THREE believes s/he is lovable only for what s/he does, not for who she is.

This God image is a bit too sleek and cool, the stainless steel kitchen God, the divine technocrat.

THREEs are trying to keep up with God, and they maintain an endless competition. While TWOs try to love more than God, THREEs try to accomplish more. They are *do-ers* and afraid to be mere human *beings*.

They find their God by running a race with him. Remember Malcolm Boyd's book, *Are You Running with Me, Jesus?* Undoubtedly he's a THREE. THREEs keep performing until they experience an *Unconditional* Lover.

The God Image of FOURs. The FOUR God is the one I mentioned in passing, the *Deus absconditus:* the hidden God, the God who has absconded and is hiding. This is God as absence.

Part of everyone's journey includes darkness, emptiness, aloneness. During these dark periods, we relate to God as absence, not just as presence. On the journey there's an interplay between the two — just as in a love-relationship. You've got to be separated from your beloved now and then to realize the new texture and shape of the relationship. You can't develop a relationship with constant presence. That's why a lot of marriages are co-dependent; there's too much presence.

The FOURs find a special power in the absence — in the longing — where, in their desiring, they move into fantasy. They move into their dream of what God should be, what God must be, what I need God to be.

Now through that very absence, they can come to a greater experience of God.

But I want to point out the false side of that God image: FOURs can get maudlin about the darkness and the absence. They don't allow God to show the divine face because that would take away their depression, which has become bittersweet to them. They like the sweetness of the bitterness: "God has tragically rejected me," they say. For the FOUR, there's something sweet about that divine rejection.

So the FOUR has to let God show the presence and the warmth. Let God show his face — or her face — or whatever face. Don't get too attached and addicted to the absence so it becomes an end in itself; otherwise you are not open to revelation and grace when it comes.

The God Image of FIVEs. The FIVEs have adopted a constantly re-curring God image from philosophy and theology: God is the Eternal Idea. In classical Greek thought, for example, God was defined as pure intelligence or divine ideas. The Greek term for that God image in John's Gospel is *Logos*, the Word.

John chose this great abstract philosophical concept for his pro-logue, because it is almost the opposite of the TWO God he is going to reveal in the rest of his Gospel — the Jesus who loves us and is crucified for us. He connects the flesh-and-blood TWO Jesus with the FIVE Logos: the abstract eternal idea, the pre-existent Christ, the Second Person of the Blessed Trinity who holds the seminal ideas of all reality within himself. The divine Logos is the pre-existent Christ, the abstract philosopher's God who explains the meaning of all things. FIVEs are comfortable with that God, the God who explains, but allows them to remain detached.

The first chapter of John's Gospel should be a FIVE's meditation, *all* of it.

The Logos was not satisfied to remain only Word, but took flesh and pitched his tent among us (John 1:14).

Many FIVEs have admitted to me that they're a bit uncomfortable with Christianity. It's too fleshy. It's too bloody. It's too specific and incarnate. It's too involved and engaged. They would rather remain absorbed with the abstract Logos than embrace the passionate flesh.

That movement into flesh, passion, and incarnation is the move-ment the FIVE must also make. God as Divine Ideas is a toxic god for them, although it's their usual starting place.

The God Image of SIXes. The SIX's God image is one we will have no trouble relating to because I think it's been the God of much religious music. It is the God you find in the Psalms of the Old Testa-ment. This is the image of God as "rock," "savior," "deliverer." Many Christian hymns emphasize "Jesus my savior."

Unfortunately, much of Christianity has been interpreted through a SIX bias, especially in this country obsessed with security. All of us Americans seem to be looking for ultimate security, a savior, a rock or deliverer who will take away our insecurity. That's why, by and large, Western religion has generated this image of conservatism — people who protect the status quo — because America has kept the SIX God in power for a long time. That is one reason Marx suggested that God and religion are the opium of the people.

Many people talk about God as one who takes away my insecurity or the one who gives me certitude. Insecurity and certitude are major SIX questions. But those questions help open up only one-ninth of the whole truth. On the religious journey, we're looking for a God who's a lot bigger. If you're attached to a God who only takes away your fears and your insecurities, you haven't met the real God. I promise you, the real God is going to lead you into deeper darkness and deeper insecurities.

So it's not enough just to be attached to a rock, a deliverer, and a savior. This is to focus on only one portion of the gospel: salvation. "How can I get saved?" As a result, it is easy for SIXes to ignore the Sermon on the Mount.

The Sermon on the Mount offers you no security and no certitudes and does not present God as a rock or a deliverer. Rather, it is leading you into dangerous uncharted territory where the ego has no control and no certitude.

Both Protestantism and Catholicism have ignored the God who upsets the status quo and takes away your certitude, the God of Abraham and Sarah, Isaac, Jacob, Jesus and Mary.

The God Image of SEVENs. The SEVEN's images clearly include God as Eternal Light, Eternal Delight, Eternal Creation, Eternal Beauty.

Their favorite feast is Easter. They prefer to focus on God coming out of the tomb, moving away from death into beauty and into glory.

But the resurrection interpreted apart from the crucifixion is only half of the paschal mystery. You can't trust an image of the risen Christ alone. SEVENs haven't met the true risen Christ until they've gone through the tomb with him. The true Risen Christ is on the other side of death.

SEVENs at their worst want the Risen Christ and the eternal light *this side of death*.

SEVENs need to realize that the God on this side of death is not the true light that has come into the world. The true light that has come into the world is Jesus who for thirty years walked on the ground, in the dirt, and died suffering on a cross.

The God Image of EIGHTs. The EIGHT God is the God that frequently appeared in classical Greek drama, the *Deus ex machina* — a dramatic invention of the author to solve an otherwise unsolvable problem. *Deus ex machina* literally means "the God who appears from a machine" to make things turn out okay in the end.

EIGHTs are waiting for this powerful God to arrive on a chariot, hoping he's going to be as powerful as they are. But they are usually disappointed in God's apparent lack of power and effectiveness. As one EIGHT told me in Kansas City, "I've always thought God was a wimp. He doesn't come through. He's not there solving the problem."

This sounds a bit like the God image of the THREE, but for EIGHTs the emphasis is more on power than efficiency. EIGHTs resent that God isn't getting things done quickly and making things happen effectively — as they see it.

For EIGHTs, God is not yet the all-powerful *Deus ex machina* of Greek drama. But they have the expectation that this is what God should be: the great problem-solver who comes in and takes care of these suffering children — or whatever the problem may be.

EIGHTs are very angry at this God image, which is quite understandable. If the only God image you have is of an all-powerful problem-solver, the Lamb of God image doesn't make a lot of sense to you.

However, if EIGHTs would go inside to their own inner child, it would open them up to other images of God. Often they finally do, and then they can meet the Lamb of God.

But mostly they want a Lion of God. They want a God who makes things happen. And they're pretty upset at the God they seem to get. He does not use his power well, and they have no patience or understanding of powerlessness.

It's not surprising that EIGHTs have a hard time with faith. They sometimes get thoroughly annoyed at religion. To them, it just doesn't appear to be doing its job or accomplishing anything.

I can imagine an EIGHT saying, "The church is not going anywhere, so I guess I gotta go out and do it. I'm gonna go do it because God just isn't doing his job." God is not playing the *Deus ex machina*. But the point I'm making is that, for EIGHTs, that's still their image of what God should be, a problem solver.

On the other hand, when they can enter into the mystery of powerlessness, which is what we symbolize by the Lamb of God, and walk with their own inner child, they meet a wholly other God who is also redeeming, also saving, also liberating, also loving. But this God's way is different from the way of power.

EIGHTs have trouble with Christianity because Jesus is portrayed as powerless. They forget that the spiritual journey involves learning power *through* powerlessness. It is difficult for them to see that Jesus the Lamb is still powerful, but power is redefined.

You can say the same for Yahweh, the God of Israel. Yahweh is the one in power who is liberating Israel, but at the same time Yahweh is identifying with Israel in its pain. This powerless God image is developed largely through the prophets and in the book of Job.

In a certain sense, EIGHTs have a real conflictual image of God. On the one hand, they want God to do their bidding; but then they don't really respect or understand God. It doesn't fit what in their minds God should be. On the other hand, they want the powerful God as *Deus ex machina*, which they'd like to respect, but they're not sure they can respect him because he's not coming through in the ways they think he should. That's why I think EIGHTs have trouble with faith.

Once they get there — like Teresa of Avila — they've got it together. God as powerful powerlessness!

Gut people move between the inner and the outer worlds and are best at integrating them. You see that in redeemed EIGHTs. They'll really have access to their inner center and their inner life, but they also know immediately how to engage it with the outer life. Call an EIGHT on an inner journey and they can do a lot of good with it.

But they do have two conflicting God images: God as weakness and God as power from above.

The God Image of NINEs. If for the FOUR, God is Absence, for the NINE, God is Presence, a quiet, constant, unquestioned Presence. It's a presence that's not demanding a lot from them, not making them jump a line of hurdles like we ONEs would expect, but just quietly present. That's why NINEs can be so nonviolent and so at home in this world.

I describe them as Adam and Eve in the Garden. There is a quiet, unarticulated, and unquestioned trust in the Presence underneath it all. "It'll work out," they say.

That image is why they don't feel they have to bust their butt like the rest of us do. NINEs say, "God's at work. It's okay."

But, NINEs, that's not the total image of God. Don't get too cozy with this God-as-presence. You need to be a bit less nonviolent and more energetic. You need to struggle with this image, articulate it a little, then get into co-creation with this Presence.

It would help if NINEs could do a little fighting with this God, wrestling like Jacob the THREE would do with his God.

To bring energy to their relationship with God will give NINEs a much more alive, active God. NINEs should not be afraid to fight with God and yell at God once in a while.

NINEs, let God be a co-participant with you — not just a quiet presence, but an active runner on the journey. Too-easy-presence is finally not presence at all, but complacency, false peace, not unlike a couple that keeps a marriage together because it is too much trouble to do anything else.

Letting Go of God Images and Self-Images

I share these reflections with you. I don't know if they're the best — listen to my ONE talking! I hope you see that we've been trapped in our number and that in each case our God is too small.

We each suffer from a partial image of God and even a conflictual or false image of God.

To move forward in faith, your God image must periodically fall apart. Your self-image must periodically fall apart as well. If you are willing to let go of both of them, you will really grow.

But it really takes faith when they both fall apart at the same time. When this happens, your God image doesn't work anymore and your self-image isn't alive or real. You hate your God image because you can't trust it, and you don't like what you are. At that point you'd better learn how to pray. Those are the dark nights of the soul, when you must pray, "Lead us not into temptation and deliver us from evil."

When the spiritual darkness begins, most people will jump back into past securities. But if you're willing to hang in there with the hidden God, if you're willing to trust and wait in hope, I promise you a new faith will be revealed and a new self will be revealed. And those two new realities will know how to live together.

They both change — self-image and God image. They have to. When one changes, the other will soon have to change. When your self-image changes, your God image has got to change. If it doesn't, you're in major dissonance. Your faith can't grow.

In the darkness, some try to hang on to their old self-image while they are willing to explore some new theology. That's false religion, when you change your religious jargon but the inner self doesn't change. I observe a lot of that dissonance in fundamentalism.

But you can equally make the mistake on the other side. You can let your self-image be changed, perhaps by doing serious inner work, yet still keep an infantile Baltimore Catechism notion of God. People who have a new and mature self-image but keep their childhood God image are the ones leaving the church. The biggest religious denomination in the United States is the Catholics: we're 26 percent of the population. Do you know what the second biggest denomination is? Ex-Catholics.

There are so many ex-Catholics because the church hasn't taught them to keep growing religiously and theologically. No one gave

them healthy adult theology or a mature image of God to keep pace
with their maturing image of themselves.

Faith and Mystery

Let me end as I began, quoting Karl Rahner:

The act of faith that it takes to accept the infinite mystery that
you are to yourself and the act of faith that it takes to accept
the infinite mystery of who God really is are finally the *same*
act of faith.

And those acts of faith move forward in parallel fashion, in my
opinion. The inner journey of contemplation calls you to the outer
journey of action and involvement. The outer journey of action and
engagement with this world drives you back to a need and desire for
contemplation.

Closing Prayer

Loving God,
we come before you with our desiring and longing,
with our desire to be co-creators with you.
We come with our guts, our hearts, and our minds
to the re-creation of this world.
You said you would give us your Spirit
to renew the face of the earth.
We ask for your Spirit for one another and for ourselves.
We ask for your Spirit for the world.

Lord, we thank you for bringing us into this world.
We realize we know only a little part of you,
and we don't have adequate names for you.
Now we know that we don't even know ourselves very well
We ask your Spirit to lead us and teach us,
and we will not be afraid.
Your perfect Love
casts out our fear, our anger,
and our abiding loneliness.
Amen.

Appendix

The Enneagram as Clue
to Who We Are

by Clarence Thomson

Occasionally throughout this book, Richard Rohr mentions people's Enneagram numbers in order to describe or predict some of their characteristics. Most of the people attending the retreat on which the book is based were versed in the Enneagram and knew their own numbers and probably the significance of other numbers as well. Not all readers may share this knowledge.

The Enneagram is a popular personality typing system. In the Enneagram theory of personality, each of us has a central compulsion or preoccupation created by our way of paying attention, of searching for or avoiding certain things in life. Each personality type has one chief characteristic, and from this central trait a whole network of smaller preferences, outlooks, and tendencies can be inferred.

Briefly, each of the nine numbers can be described in a thumbnail sketch. This sketch is less than an introduction to the Enneagram, but it will explain a bit why Father Rohr makes the allusions — often light-hearted ones — to particular numbers in a particular context.

Type ONE, which Rohr acknowledges he himself is, is the moral perfectionist and ethical reformer. ONEs tend to have an unacknowledged anger, to be critical, especially of themselves, and to see life as a theater for moral heroism.

Type TWO is the quintessential helper, who goes through life meeting other people's needs while not acknowledging his or her own needs. TWOs are the most interpersonal of all the types, being largely concerned about the quality of relationships at all times. If they are needy, they can't admit it, so they have a tendency to become manipulative. If healthy, they are sweet, almost seductive, and unbelievably forgiving.

Type THREE is the success-oriented, high-energy, super-achiever that is the American hero. THREEs put their emotional needs on hold and try to win love through performance. They are socially astute, being able to project the image of whatever it is the situation needs. If unhealthy, they are unfeeling workaholics. If healthy, they get in touch with love and other personal values.

Type FOUR is the tragic romantic artistic type. FOURs like to be with other FOURs (in artists' colonies, for example) because they feel no one else can really understand the depth of their emotions. Their compulsion is to be different, special, to be authentic and take the emotional component of life more seriously than the rest of life. They have a curious ability to wallow in pain, feeling that pain has the power to make them emotionally deeper than others.

Type FIVE is the detached, observant, intellectual who approaches life as a spectacle to be watched. These are the people who get labelled "ivory tower" types because they prefer to keep their distance from the hurly-burly of life and reflect on it instead. The academic world is full of FIVE professors who specialize in footnotes. When healthy they are the finest of thinkers and researchers and have an unequalled intellectual depth.

Type SIX is the fearful person who sees every situation in terms of what could go wrong. SIXes are ambivalent about authority, both fiercely loyal and suspicious of it. They love keeping the group together (family, team, order, any group) and so tend to want all the laws enforced so nobody in the group strays from the center.

Type SEVENs are fun-loving, high-energy persons who often have a problem growing up because they avoid pain with too much ardor. If unhealthy, they are addicted to any kind of pleasure — food, sex, drugs, enjoyable work, art — and tend to be dilettantes. If healthy, they become renaissance persons because of their wide range of interests and vitality.

Type EIGHT is the person who considers the world to be about power. EIGHTs are enormously powerful themselves; they scorn weakness and constantly put pressure on people to see if they will crack. Paradoxically, they are the champions of the underdogs in their world and devote huge amounts of time and talent seeing to it that the little ones get justice.

Type NINEs are the peace-seekers of the world. They want no conflict and so they keep a low emotional profile, not committing themselves to any position until all turmoil related to it is over. They are the most passive-aggressive, people-pleasing among the Enneagram types. Their problem is a certain spiritual indolence. They may work hard to cover up the fact they are not taking care of the central spiritual concerns of their lives.

Even though it is necessary to describe probable behaviors, the real heart of the Enneagram is one layer deeper. The nine types are really nine energies. Nine motives. Nine worldviews. Any number can do anything, but the reasons for doing it will be different.

Clarence Thomson is editor of the Enneagram Educator, *based in Kansas City.* This appendix also appeared in Richard Rohr, *Quest for the Holy Grail* (New York: Crossroad, 1994).

Index

OTHER BOOKS BY

RICHARD ROHR

DISCOVERING THE ENNEAGRAM
An Ancient Tool for a New Spiritual Journey
0-8245-1185-9; $14.95 paperback

EXPERIENCING THE ENNEAGRAM
0-8245-1201-4; $14.95 paperback

QUEST FOR THE GRAIL
Soul Work and the Sacred Journey
0-8245-1654-0; $14.95 paperback

SIMPLICITY
The Art of Living
0-8245-1251-0; $11.95 paperback

JOB AND THE MYSTERY OF SUFFERING
0-8245-1474-2; $19.95 hardcover

THE GOOD NEWS ACCORDING TO LUKE
Spiritual Reflections
0-8245-1490-7; $19.95 hardcover

Please support your local bookstore, or call 1-800-395-0690.
For a free catalog, please write us at
THE CROSSROAD PUBLISHING COMPANY
370 LEXINGTON AVENUE, NEW YORK, NY 10017

We hope you enjoyed Enneagram II. *Thank you for reading it.*

crossroad